GUERNSEY COUNTRY DIARY

Cover: Stonechat on gorse at L'Ancresse;
Overleaf: Curlew – see October

Guernsey Country Diary

Through the Natural Year with
Nigel Jee

Illustrations by Justine Peek

Seaflower Books

Published in 1997 by
Seaflower Books
1 The Shambles
Bradford on Avon
Wiltshire

Design and typesetting by Ex Libris Press

Cover printed by
Shires Press, Trowbridge, Wiltshire

Printed and bound by
Cromwell Press, Broughton Gifford, Wiltshire

ISBN 0 948578 90 4

J a n u a r y

It is surprising how often the year opens with a cold snap. The weather at Christmas is usually soft and mild, with no hint of what is to come. On the cliffs ox-eye daisy and red campion are in bloom, and in the garden there are jasmine, forsythia, wych hazel and *Iris stylosa.*

For some years I have been counting the flowers in the garden on or around New Year's Day. In the last ten years the number of species in bloom has varied between 58 and 83. This includes not only cultivated plants, but weeds as well – at this time of year any flower is welcome, whether official or otherwise.

Now, just as the days are at last beginning to lengthen we have fallen into the clutches of a continental high pressure system, with its frost and snow. Suddenly the garden is full of redwings. They are hopping about everywhere, probing the lawn for

Above: Redwing, a regular winter visitor

worms, tearing up the 'mind-your-own-business' which forms a green carpet at the edge of the grass, and scattering it all over the path. The energetic way in which they flick leaves aside in their search for small animals reminds me of the turnstones on the beach, scattering seaweed in pursuit of sandhoppers.

Nearly every winter the island is invaded by flocks of lapwings, fieldfares and redwings, escaping from hard weather further north. Lapwings prefer large fields and open areas. They are particularly fond of the airport, and a flock can nearly always be seen somewhere near the runway during cold winter weather. Fieldfares and redwings form mixed flocks, but the fieldfare prefers more open country than the redwing, and is less inclined to come close to human dwellings. So it is mainly redwings that are making themselves at home in our garden and the surrounding fields.

The redwing is the smallest common European thrush. It is not unlike our resident song thrush, but is slightly smaller, with a darker back. It is easily distinguished by its conspicuous creamy-white eye stripe and chestnut flanks. It breeds in woodland and arctic scrub in Scandinavia, the Baltic and Siberia, and spends the winter in central and southern Europe and the Mediterranean. We regularly see redwings as they move between the two areas in spring and autumn. The birds that pass through Guernsey probably remain close to the west coast of Europe; an indication of this is that in the last few years six redwings, ringed in Guernsey, have been recovered in Portugal. Winter influxes such as we are seeing at present, however, are nothing to do with this regular migration, but are purely the result of hard weather on the continent.

For the last few nights there have been frosts, and today the temperature remained below freezing point all day – a rare event in this island. The redwings, unable to extract worms or woodlice from the frozen ground, have turned their attention to the berries. Until now the resident blackbirds and thrushes have been able to find animal food in abundance, and they have left the berries for a rainy day. Now suddenly pyracantha, cotoneaster and those holly berries that survived Christmas are attracting the redwings. Even rose hips, usually the last to go, are disappearing.

In a misguided moment about ten years ago we planted the rampageous rose 'Kiftsgate'. The intention was to grow it into an old cypress tree which has lost its lower branches, and needs brightening up. This it resolutely refused to do. Instead, it romped across the head of the well, joined another rose clinging to the wall of the barn, ran the whole length of the barn and jumped into a large lilac tree at the other end, from where it tries periodically to get in through our bedroom window. Now the lilac flowers are succeeded each summer by large, round heads of cream 'Kiftsgate' flowers, with yellow stamens. The flowers are followed by small, bullet-like hips which the birds won't touch unless conditions are serious. Such conditions have obviously arrived, for the redwings have cleared the lot.

It is the first ormering tide of the year, and the powers that be have asked us to give it a miss. Turning over the boulders on the shoreline would expose not only ormers, but all the other marine life, to the biting wind and frost. It might be thought that it would have the same effect on the ormer gatherer, but there are still plenty of Guernseymen who will wade happily into the icy water at low spring tides in the winter, in search of the delectable mollusc. The trouble is there are not as many ormers as there used to be.

The ormer is closely related to the limpet, but the shell is ear-shaped (hence the name, a contraction of *oreille de mer*). The shell is pierced by a row of holes. Five of these are usually open, the older ones being sealed over as fast as new ones are formed at the growing edge of the shell. Sea water which has passed over the gills is discharged through the holes, together with eggs, sperms and waste matter. The edible part, which is prized as a delicacy, is the flat, muscular foot. With this the animal can move over the rocks at a surprising speed, or hang on tenaciously if it is exposed at low tide.

It has to be said that ormers are on the tough side. Having cut away the rest of the animal and scrubbed the foot, it is usually given a good beating to soften it up. Then, fried with plenty of onions and left to stew slowly all night in a casserole, there is nothing to touch it.

The population of ormers has always been vulnerable, for in the Channel Islands the species is at the extreme edge of its geographical range. It is an animal of the Mediterranean, which extends up the Atlantic coast of Europe just as far as these islands. The numbers on the shore have always fluctuated, but there has been a dramatic decline since the war, caused partly by over-fishing, and partly by a slight fall in the average temperature of the water.

Ormer, a threatened delicacy

The main population lives well below the low-tide mark, and in the past the ormers collected at low tide by shore gatherers were soon replaced from deeper water. In the 1960s many thousands of ormers were collected by divers and exported, and fewer and fewer were left to recolonise the shore. Today diving for ormers is banned in all the islands, and they may only be collected from the shore at certain spring tides in the winter. They must be at least three inches in length.

Nothing can be done about the temperature of the water. It is in the breeding process that this is critical. Eggs and sperms, having been ejected through the holes in the shell, float in the water and the sperms have to find the eggs in the vast body of the sea. The fertilised eggs develop into minute swimming larvae, which eventually settle on the bottom and start feeding on the seaweed encrusting the rocks.

This all needs a minimum temperature very close to that around Guernsey. Adults can live and grow in colder water, and young ormers from Guernsey have been successfully grown on in Galway Bay. At present they cannot breed naturally north of the English Channel, but these things go in cycles, and perhaps one of the happier effects of global warming will be to bring ormers back onto the menu, not only in Guernsey, but across the Channel as well.

After several gloomy days of cold, damp fog the sun has at last broken through, and already in the fields and beside the cliff paths the first celandine flowers are opening. Strictly speaking the delightful spring flower is the lesser celandine, to distinguish it from the much rarer greater celandine, which flowers in the summer. The two are not related; the lesser celandine belongs to the buttercup family, while the greater is a poppy. The only thing they have in common is the yellow colour of the petals.

The golden, star-shaped flowers of the lesser celandine open on sunny days, and turn to face the sun. If you stand with your back to the sun, so that the light is reflected from the flowers, the effect of a bank of celandines can be quite dazzling. But it will be February or March before the display is at its height. At present only one or two flowers have dared to open.

If a celandine plant is dug up it can be seen that the root system consists of a bunch of white fig-shaped tubers. The herbalists of the middle ages thought they resembled haemorrhoids, and took this to be a sign that the plant could be used to cure this unfortunate affliction. For this reason one of the English names of the plant is pilewort. In Guernsey French the plant is *pisse-en-lliet*. Why the lesser celandine should be associated in Guernsey with bed-wetting is a mystery. In France *pissenlit* is the dandelion, and in England also it is the dandelion that has that reputation.

Although the flowers are only now beginning to appear, the heart-shaped leaves have been abundant among the grass for several weeks. They are beautifully marbled in various shades of green, and in our orchard some of the plants have bronze leaves.

Celandine

Many of the celandine leaves contain contorted white tunnels, excavated by leaf-miners. These are the larvae of a fly which lays its eggs in the leaves. Each egg hatches into a grub which eats its way through the juicy middle layer, leaving the upper and lower coverings of the leaf intact. As the grub grows the mine becomes broader, until finally the grub pupates. After a few days the adult fly emerges from the pupa, eats its way to the surface and flies away. If an infected leaf is held up to the light the pupa, or an empty pupa case, can be seen as a dark, oval object at the thick end of the mine.

There are several species of leaf-miner, each favouring a different plant or group of plants. In our garden we notice them particularly in the summer on honeysuckle and hogweed. They are welcome to the hogweed, which gives me a rash every time I touch it, and defies all attempts at eradication. Unfortunately the leaf-miners don't seem to do it any harm either. The leaf-miner most in evidence at this time of year, however, is the one that goes for buttercups and lesser celandine.

One of the delights of a walk in the lanes at this time of year is the sweet vanilla scent of winter heliotrope, which is flowering now beside the road in many parts of the island. The spikes of pale mauve flowers have been blooming since before Christmas, and now the horseshoe-shaped leaves are beginning to appear.

The plant, from Mediterranean North Africa, was introduced into Britain as a garden flower in 1806. Its main attraction was its winter scent. It proved to be too successful, spreading to form dense masses and killing off other plants, so it was evicted from gardens and soon became thoroughly naturalised in waste places and on roadside banks. One of the first records of the plant growing wild in the British Isles was in 1838, when C.C. Babington saw it in Guernsey.

Because of the shape of the leaf, the name of the plant in Guernsey French is *pas d'âne*, although in Guernsey English it is usually referred to as coltsfoot. This can cause confusion, for the name coltsfoot properly belongs to a different plant, rarely seen in Guernsey, with yellow, dandelion-like flowers.

Large patches of winter heliotrope are so widespread that it comes as a surprise to find that the plant relies for its propagation entirely on its creeping underground stems. It produces no seed in Guernsey, for male and female flowers are borne on separate plants, and all our plants are male.

❋

When do frogs begin to spawn? I posed this question a year or two ago in the local paper, and received an astonishing number of replies. Frogs are obviously much-loved animals and, in spite of their diminishing habitat, there still seem to be a fair number about.

In the United Kingdom the average date of spawning varies from late April in the extreme north to late February in the south. In the far south-west of England it often takes place in early February. In Guernsey some spawning certainly takes place in February, but several people regularly have spawn in their garden ponds in January, or even in late December. My grandchildren claim to have seen frog spawn on Christmas Eve, again in a garden pond.

The number of reports involving garden ponds shows how important these have become to frogs, now that so many of the marshy areas where they used to live have been drained or developed. But frogs are conservative creatures, and it may take many years to change their habits. Frogs return to the pond where they were born to breed. When a pond was filled in and grassed over at the old girls' grammar school at Rosaire Avenue, the frogs continued to return to it, and the following year in desperation they left their spawn on the grass. It is certainly worth the trouble of providing the frogs with a breeding place in the garden, for they are expert at dealing with slugs and snails.

Most, if not all, of the frogs seen today in Guernsey are common frogs, so called because this is the common species in England. But the continental agile frog has certainly been in the island until recently, and may well still be here. The two species are difficult to tell apart. The agile frog has a finer, more pointed snout, and longer legs, with which it is supposed to be able to leap further. Perhaps the best distinction in the position of the heels when the frog is squatting in its usual resting posture. In the common frog they are in line with the rear of the body, while in the agile frog they project behind it.

Frog

Jersey is supposed to have only agile frogs, and in 1988 naturalists in that island were dismayed when someone released some common frogs into the wild. Because of the drainage and pollution of swamps the agile frog is becoming rare, and there was a danger that the newcomer may oust it from its few remaining marshes. The offending animals were rounded up and sent to Guernsey, where it was felt they would be more at home. In 1990 the same thing happened, and again the aliens were sent to Guernsey. Common frogs still occasionally turn up in Jersey. But both species live happily side by side in the neighbouring parts of France, often breeding and croaking lustily in the same ponds. Let us hope that we can retain enough ponds and swampy areas in Guernsey to allow both species to survive here.

F e b r u a r y

The rabbits must be starving. For some years we have not allowed shooting in our fields, and now we are paying the price. When the ground was covered in snow last month they invaded the garden and ate the Brussels sprouts. Not just the sprouts, but the whole plants down to the stumps. They didn't like the spinach, but we don't particularly like it either. Now they have retreated back to the fields, where they have mown the grass like a bowling green.

The trouble with rabbits is that they nibble the grass so close to the ground that they eat out the growing buds. The useful grasses then die, and are replaced by weeds such as chickweed, which even the rabbits won't eat.

Rabbits were introduced in the middle ages, and kept in warrens or *garennes*. One, La Garenne d'Anneville, still exists in

Above: Rabbit

St. Sampson's. They were an important source of fresh meat, and the *garennes* were closely guarded from poachers. This did not prevent the rabbits from escaping, and they have been multiplying in the manner for which they are famous ever since.

Being an introduced animal, there is no efficient predator. The cats do their best, and in the morning we often find half a rabbit on the mat. It is always the back half. The head is the best part as far as the cats are concerned, even if they have to spit out the teeth. Kestrels take a few young rabbits, and there are ferrets which have gone missing and become feral, but none of these make any significant difference to the rabbit population. When pushed beyond the limit I have been known to grab a gun and go out with murder in my heart, but when the rabbit just sits and looks at you, what can you do?

Fortunately even the rabbits can't eat daffodils. The young, dark green leaves are coming up strongly in the fields, and already the first blooms are beginning to open. The daffs are relics of the days when bulbs were grown commercially. At the end of the last century and the first half of this, Guernsey used to compete with the Isles of Scilly in sending the flowers to London as early in the year as possible, to catch the best market. When we first came to this house in the 1950s we would pick them, bunch them and pack them in boxes for Covent Garden, but after a few years the freight charges became more than the flowers were worth. They still come up year after year, but now we simply enjoy them where they are.

The earliest varieties are the multi-headed scented narcissi derived from Mediterranean species. Already the pure white 'Paperwhite' and the golden 'Soleil d'Or' have begun to flower, and soon the cream coloured 'Grand Primo' will join them. But this year 'Grand Primo' has been beaten by the yellow trumpet daffodil 'Golden Spur'. This is one of many old varieties which were exported in vast quantities earlier in the century. Later in the spring, when 'Golden Spur' has finished flowering, it will be replaced in our fields by 'Emperor' and 'Sir Watkin', two varieties which are often open at the right moment for decorating the church at Easter.

The true wild daffodil or Lent lily, which grows on the cliffs and in the wooded valleys of Jersey, is unknown in Guernsey. All our 'wild' daffodils are old cultivated varieties, which persist in the fields and hedges, digging themselves deeper and deeper into the soil every year. Many of the inland valleys have terraces where bulbs were once grown. Today they are overgrown with brambles and bracken, but beneath the undergrowth the daffodils still come up each year, along with bluebells and the white bells of three-cornered garlic.

Some of the most interesting varieties are in the hedges between fields, for when bulbs were grown as a crop, any that proved to be the 'wrong' variety were pulled up and thrown into the hedge, where they took root and flourished. Well over fifty old cultivated varieties of daffodil have been found naturalised in Guernsey. Many have been named; others have lived longer than the people who could have named them. The hedges and overgrown terraces are a living museum of these old varieties.

The fourteenth of February is the Feast of St. Valentine. Nobody knows why the third-century Roman martyr should have become associated with lovers. Probably the only connection is that his feast-day is also the day on which the birds are supposed to choose their mates – a tradition which goes back at least as far as Chaucer.

Many of the birds around here seem to have jumped the gun. For some days a pair of kestrels have been chasing each other among the chimneys, squealing with excitement, and two robins have been feeding together at the bird table – an unthinkable event if they were not a pair. Blue tits are the most frequent visitors to the bird table at present, but they will not begin brooding until March. We normally have one or two pairs breeding in holes in the wall somewhere in the garden, but just now we seem to be feeding the tits from a much wider area.

The winter flocks of starlings are breaking up, and some seem to be taking up residence in the garden. We can recognise some individual birds by quirks in their song. Judging by the wisps of hay hanging from the eaves of the barn, at least one pair of starlings has begun to build under the gutter. A pair of feral pigeons, which have arrived uninvited and taken up residence in a pigeon hole in the gable of the house, have also been active. A few mornings ago I found an empty egg-shell on the ground beneath their hole. They are welcome to make use of our facilities as long as they don't eat the vegetables. So far they have been going out for their meals – somebody, somewhere, must be feeding them.

The bantams have been laying ever since the days began to lengthen in January, and now one of the hens has disappeared. This almost certainly means she is sitting on a clutch of eggs somewhere in the undergrowth, and in three weeks time she will reappear with a family of chicks.

Now is the time to look for the Guernsey fern. This immensely rare hybrid, which as far as we know is unique to Guernsey, grows in shady hedgebanks in the southern half of the island. At other times of year it hides among the vegetation and is almost impossible to find, but in January and February the glossy, evergreen leaves are exposed to view.

The Guernsey fern is a cross between two fairly common hedgerow ferns: lanceolate spleenwort and hart's-tongue. Hart's-tongue is easy to find, for it has long, strap-shaped leaves which are not divided like those of other ferns into feathery segments. It grows luxuriantly in damp, shady places, the fronds sometimes reaching three feet in length. Lanceolate spleenwort is a more typically 'fern-like' fern, which grows unobtrusively in shady hedges, especially where there is some bare soil.

The hybrid, as you would expect, looks like a mixture of both parents. The fronds are cut into segments, but these are not feathery. Instead they are broad, wavy and overlap each other. It is a striking plant which, once seen, is never forgotten. It is not unlike the sea spleenwort which grows in rock crevices around the coast, and at first it was thought to be a variety of this fern. But it has since been proved to be a hybrid between the two hedgerow parents.

The Guernsey fern was first discovered in St. Pierre-du-Bois in 1855, and the following year one was found in Cornwall. About a dozen plants were subsequently found in the west of Guernsey, but there is no confirmed record of it having been seen again in England. The Guernsey plants eventually died, or were dug up (for this was the height of the Victorian fern craze), and the hybrid was not seen again until 1965, when it was rediscovered by Peter Girard, then headmaster of the Castel School.

Peter was already well known for his botanical serendipity, but on this occasion he surpassed himself. He was riding his horse through a densely shaded lane in the Castel parish, when he noticed a fern which was different from anything he had seen before. He sent a piece to the British Museum, who confirmed it as the hybrid not seen since the last century. Since then a number of plants of the Guernsey fern have been seen in different parts of the island, but always in shady hedgebanks. At present about ten are known to be alive.

If so many plants have appeared in Guernsey, why does it not grow anywhere else? One reason is that Guernsey is one of the few places where the two parents meet. In the UK hart's-tongue grows mainly on limy soils, and is frost-hardy, while lanceolate spleenwort is limited to the mild south-west and needs an acid soil. For some reason the two grow happily side by side in Guernsey, where the high hedgebanks, shaded by trees, provide exactly the right conditions for both parents and the hybrid to flourish.

The ants are on the march in the kitchen. They have spent the winter deep in the wall somewhere, and every year at about this time they send out a party of scouts to see if it is time to wake up. If they find the smallest crumb of an edible nature they hurry back to tell their friends, and in no time the kitchen is full of the highly organised creatures.

The ants belong to a continental species which is not found in the UK, and has no English name. Its scientific name is *Lasius emarginatus*. It is related to the black English garden ant, but differs in its colouring: our ant has a dark brown head and tail, but the middle section of the body is light brown. It is common in gardens and old houses in the Channel Islands, and tends to upset householders who are not used to it. But it does not bite or sting, does no harm, and efficiently clears up crumbs which might otherwise be overlooked. When it is warmer outside the ants will disappear from the kitchen as suddenly as they came, and for the rest of the summer we will see them foraging in the garden. Then, perhaps on a thundery day in August, they will swarm and disperse.

Ants find their way and recognise each other by smell. Each colony has its characteristic scent, and when a route to some food has been established, the ants blindly follow the scent left by the feet of their comrades. Soon there is a highway, with ants hurrying in both directions. Often this is in a dark corner where the ants attract no attention. But when it crosses a working surface, my wife gets active with the soap and water. This removes the scent, and soon the kitchen is full of confused ants trying to find their way home.

Whenever two ants meet they touch antennae, and if the other smells of a different colony, there is a fight. On one occasion two different colonies appeared at opposite ends of the kitchen, and advanced towards each other. When we came down in the morning there must have been a decisive battle, for the floor was littered with corpses. I assured my wife that if we left them they would all disappear, for ants do not believe in wasting good meat. But she lacks the spirit of scientific enquiry, and insisted on sweeping them up.

✪

The short-toed treecreeper is a delightful resident bird, to be seen at any time of year, working its way spirally up the trunk of a tree and winkling spiders and insects out of cracks in the bank with its long, slender, curved bill. It is a small, self-effacing, mouse-like bird with brown back and pale greyish underparts. In the summer it is difficult to see among the foliage but at this time of year it is more easily seen. As it probes the bark it uses its stiff tail to prop itself against the tree. It works rapidly, in

sporadic bursts of activity, always upwards, and when it reaches the top of one tree it flies to the bottom of the next. Its name in Guernsey French is *eppluque-poummier*, the apple-tree plucker.

The short-toed treecreeper is the only one of our breeding birds that does not also breed in the UK. It is found in all the Channel Islands, and in the lowland parts of continental Europe. It differs from the British treecreeper in having shorter toes, a longer bill and darker flanks. It also has a fuller song. But these differences are very small, and the best way to identify a treecreeper is by where you see

Treecreeper

it. If it is in Guernsey it is safe to say it will be a short-toed treecreeper. The British species has been recorded here, but only on two or three occasions, when the birds concerned must have been seriously lost.

Treecreepers build their nests in small hollows between the branches of a tree, or between thick ivy and the trunk. A few years ago a pair nested and raised a large family in a very small hole in a cypress tree in our garden. The following year the hole had grown too small for them. We still see the little birds spiralling up the cypress tree, as well as oak, ash, willow, elm and even the myrtle tree on the lawn. Doubtless they have a nest somewhere, but it is well concealed.

Crocus buds have been waiting to open for over a week now, but as the petals only open in bright, sunny weather, the buds are still waiting. It is quite mild, but a series of depressions is coming at us from the Atlantic, bringing rain, hail and gales. Snowdrops open whatever the weather, and they are at their best, while a few sweet violets and primroses are in bloom.

Beside the cliff path, and in short turf near the coast, the white flowers of Danish scurvy-grass are beginning to open. A diminutive member of the cabbage family, the flower has four small white petals, sometimes tinged with pink. The tiny, spade-shaped leaves are fleshy, and rich in ascorbic acid or vitamin C, the factor which prevents scurvy. In the 16th century sailors took the various species of scurvy-grass with them on their long voyages of discovery, but they taste pretty unpleasant, and as soon as citrus fruits became available they were used instead.

Danish scurvy-grass is a coastal plant, growing along the Atlantic fringe of Europe from Portugal to Norway. Its natural habitat is shingle, dune and cliff-top, where there is no coarse vegetation to smother it. It is tolerant of salt, and will cheerfully grow within reach of sea spray. In England it began to spread inland along the major roads in the 1980s. It particularly likes the central reservation of motorways, where it thrives on the salt which is spread in icy weather. In Guernsey it grows all round the coast, but it has also spread inland, where it grows on walls and roof tops, and on closely trimmed hedgebanks. It is an overwintering annual, the seeds germinating in the autumn. During the winter a mat of tiny leaves appears, and now the white flowers are opening one by one. Soon the banks and walls, and even the hollows in pantile roofs, will be white with the massed flowers.

Scurvy grass, a rich source of vitamin C

M a r c h

I am not sure whether March came in like a lamb or a lion – it was more like a wet sheep. Until now any rain that has fallen has been absorbed by the soil, and the water table has remained stubbornly low all through the winter. Now, at last, the soil is saturated and the water table is rising towards its normal winter level. There are puddles on the paths, and water is standing in the furrow where I have been digging the garden. No more digging until the soil dries out a bit.

The spring migration is just beginning. This month and next, thousands of birds which have spent the winter in Africa and around the Mediterranean will pass through the island on their way to their breeding grounds in the north. The first migrant to be seen was a wheatear, hopping about in search of beetles and snails on L'Ancresse Common at the beginning of the month.

Above: Little Egret, Lihou in background.

The wheatear is a rather smart member of the thrush family. The colour of the plumage varies according to the sex and time of year, but a wheatear can always be recognised because in both sexes the rump and sides of the tail are a conspicuous white. By the time of the autumn migration both sexes are a sandy brown, which camouflages them against the dry turf of the common. But always there is the white rump, exposed when the bird flies.

It flits restlessly about over the short turf of the commons and cliff-tops, keeping close to the ground, and sometimes settling on a rock, fanning its tail and bobbing.

Wheatear on L'Ancresse Common

Wheatears spend the winter in tropical Africa, and visit us in an extended migration lasting from March until June. The latecomers are birds which are on their way to Greenland, Iceland and the Arctic. Sometimes a few decide to spend the summer with us, and occasionally they have bred here, building a loose nest of grass and moss, often in a rabbit hole or among an outcrop of rocks. The great majority, however, stay for a week or two and then move on.

Wheatears have become less abundant in recent years, probably because the short downland turf which they favour is decreasing in Britain and Europe. But in spring and autumn there are still plenty to be seen at L'Ancresse and on Herm Common, and on the cliffs or any open space where there is short turf grazed by rabbits. They are delightful birds, and evocative of the wilder and more remote parts of the island.

Soon after the arrival of the wheatear, on almost the first mild, sunny day of spring, I heard my first chiffchaff singing in the treetops. The chiffchaff is a tiny, inconspicuous greenish-buff warbler, and if it were not for its song and habits, it would be almost impossible to distinguish it from the closely related willow warbler, which arrives a few days later. The song of the willow warbler is a melodious, descending scale of notes, sung from the lower branches of trees and bushes. The chiffchaff sings from the tops of the trees, and simply repeats 'chiff-chaff-chiff-chaff' – over and over again. It is a cheerful, if monotonous, sound, and a sure sign that spring has arrived.

By the end of the month chiffchaffs will be pouring through the island, and on warm sunny days every wood and valley will be full of their song. Most will move on, but many will stay for the summer and breed. Although they feed and sing in the tops of the trees, chiffchaffs breed quite close to the ground. The nest, of leaves and moss, lined with feathers, is hidden in a bramble bush or in the undergrowth of an old quarry. While the hen incubates the eggs, the cock sings from the treetops. In August he gets a sore throat and falls silent, but singing is resumed in the autumn, before the birds return to the Mediterranean. A few may stay for the winter; in mild weather the song can be heard at any time.

Very few willow warblers stay to breed. Those that do, build a domed nest of moss and grasses on the ground, among long vegetation.

Suddenly spring is here. In the field the daffodils are dancing against a background of dark green grass, and where the turf has been grazed closely, the ground is covered with the golden stars of celandine. Fat horse chestnut buds are bursting, and the elder bushes have already put out new shoots.

In the hedges and on the cliffs, blackthorn is beginning to bloom. The pure white flowers usually begin to appear on the bare branches around the middle of March. First some of the more sheltered hedges inland have a dusting of white, and later it spreads to the cliffs and commons. On the cliffs large areas in the less precipitous places are covered with almost impenetrable blackthorn scrub, and by the end of the month they will be white with blossom. In Herm, blackthorn scrub covers a considerable proportion of the island. As the boat approaches the harbour at this time of year the visitor is greeted by acres of blossom on the slopes all around. Sometimes from as far away as Guernsey the cliffs of the smaller islands appear to be covered with snow. Then the petals are brought down by a shower of rain, and the distant cliffs revert to their usual purple-grey.

We have planted quite a lot of blackthorn to thicken up our hedges in the last few years. It is an ideal hedging shrub, for its roots spread and send up suckers, filling any gaps in the hedge and developing into an impenetrable, spiny barrier. After flowering the small, oval leaves develop and the shrub becomes an inconspicuous part of the hedge until the autumn, when the purple-black sloes cover the bushes. Although blackthorn is closely related to the domestic damson, sloes are far too sour to eat – until, that is, they have been made into sloe gin. When you have drunk the gin you will find that the sloes lying at the bottom of the bottle have become quite palatable.

We are having trouble with pigeons. Not wood pigeons, or even collared doves, but feral pigeons of the Trafalgar Square variety.

Honest wild wood pigeons are no trouble, unless we forget to cover the young peas with wire. They build their untidy nests of twigs in the trees, and we can tell which branches they roost on at night by the accumulation of droppings on the ground below. Otherwise they keep out of the way except to pick up acorns from the drive, or excavate for wild garlic bulbs among the grass. To both of these they are welcome.

Collared doves are likewise no problem, though at one time it looked as if they would become a pest. These dapper little pigeons, with a black partial collar over the neck, tapering to nothing at the sides, probably originated in India. During the course of the century they have been spreading steadily westward, reaching France in 1950. In Guernsey the first collared dove was seen in 1962, and by 1964 it was breeding in some of the town gardens. The following year a pair built a nest in a sycamore tree immediately outside the window of the biology lab at Elizabeth College, where I was teaching at the time. The private life of the unfamiliar birds caused a good deal of interest, but unfortunately the publicity proved too much for them, and they did not use the nest.

Collared doves increased rapidly and were soon becoming a nuisance in farmyards and chicken runs. Then, as so often happens, they settled down and now maintain a reasonable population. In our garden a pair must be nesting somewhere, for they often sit on the television aerial cooing to each other, or make a much less melodious screech as they glide to the ground.

The feral pigeons are much more of a problem. It all started when we had to re-roof part of the house. High in the gable of the house is a pair of ventilation holes, and inside one of these is a box in which a pair of barn owls nest and roost. I thought the owls might object to the work going on so close to them, so I made a similar hole in the gable of an outbuilding, and built an owls' palace inside it.

In the event the owls decided to stay where they were, and a pair of pigeons moved into the palace. The word quickly spread among their friends and relations, and in no time there were pigeons investigating every feature of the house for possible nesting sites. They found the chimneys particularly desirable, and seemed to think that if they dropped enough sticks down them they would eventually build up to provide a comfortable nest. We lit a few fires to discourage this, and most of them seem to have found nesting holes where they are not liable to be kippered.

One particularly tame pair are convinced that the only possible place for a nest is inside the barn, just above the spot where I keep the car. As pigeons generate an incredible number of droppings I am not in favour of this, but when I shut them out of the barn they retaliated by coming in through an open window and leaving their droppings on the bed.

I don't know where this will end. A fat pigeon would provide a nice meal for a cat, but the cats have been so intimidated by the bantams that they will not go near any large bird. We may have to interfere with the balance of nature and take action ourselves.

Now that the plants are burgeoning and there is lush new growth everywhere, it is possible to take stock of the damage caused by the January frosts. The minimum temperature was – 4°C: hardly a severe frost by English standards, but an unusual occurrence here. All the native wild plants came through it unscathed, and the wild flowers are already beginning to bloom in the hedges. In the garden the pelargoniums (the ordinary tender 'geraniums' which survive outside here in a normal winter) are all stone dead. So are the Madeiran geraniums. This is a major blow, for we have come to rely on these splendid plants for a splash of vivid colour in the early summer. There are plenty of seedlings, for Madeiran geraniums are extremely prolific, but it will be two or three years before they flower.

In the first two years the plant grows into a bush about three feet tall, with large, feathery, palmate leaves on strong stalks. When it decides to flower, usually in its third year, the leaf stalks bend down to act as props which support the weight of a massive head of flowers. It is extremely spectacular, and always attracts attention when it is in bloom. My wife is less enthusiastic about it, for sometimes the props give way and it sprawls along the ground, smothering all the other plants.

The other exotic plants which always command attention are the giant echiums, or rocket plants, from Tenerife. These also seed themselves prolifically and take two or three years to reach maturity. Then in early spring the plant starts to shoot upwards, producing a slender, tapering spire fifteen or twenty feet high, covered with mauve flowers which are a magnet for bumble bees. Giant echiums are hardier than Madeiran geraniums. They looked slightly sick during the frosty weather, and for a day or two their leaves drooped to the ground. But they made a full recovery, and already the columns of flower buds are beginning to thrust upwards.

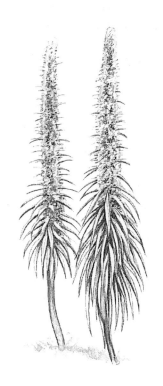

Exotic plants like giant echium and Madeiran geranium do so well in Guernsey, and seed themselves so freely, that we might expect them to escape from gardens and become naturalised, in the same way as the St. Peter Port daisy (from Mexico) and three-cornered garlic (from the Mediterranean) did in the last century. So far, however, they

Giant Echium, an introduction from Tenerife

have always been cut back after a year or two by frost. Global warming will have to go a step further before the cliffs are covered by echium spires, or the inland valleys by purple mounds of geraniums.

❁

A sign that global warming is beginning to have an effect can be seen just down the road from here, at Albecq, where a little egret has made its home for most of the past winter. The small heron is pure white, with a long, slender neck and two very long crest feathers streaming from behind the head. At low tide it stalks slowly among the rocks, or stands motionless in rock pools, in a typically heron-like manner. At high water it rests on an offshore rock, sometimes in the company of grey herons.

The little egret used to be confined in Europe to the Mediterranean region; I remember how excited I was to see my first in the Camargue in the 1950s. Even twenty years ago it was a great rarity as far north as Guernsey. Then it began to extend its range up the Atlantic coast of France. It first nested in Brittany in 1984, and there is now a regular breeding colony in the Morbihan. Since then it has continued its spread into Normandy and it is now regularly seen in the Channel Islands.

In Guernsey the occasional little egret has been seen in the spring and autumn for some years, but it was not until 1993 that a party remained for the summer on the west coast. Now they are a regular sight, both on the coast and the marshy areas inland. They have not yet attempted to breed, but it is an exciting thought that they might one day do so. In the Mediterranean lands they breed socially, often with other herons. If there are trees or shrubs close to their feeding grounds, they nest in the tops of these. There are very few places left in Guernsey that would be suitable, but there are still a few *marais* areas inland from the west coast, where thickets of sallow could support a small colony.

If grey herons ever nested in Guernsey (and there is a place near Delancey called Heronnière Lane) they ceased to do so many years ago. Perhaps their smaller cousins the little egrets will take their place.

✷

In the hedges and on the cliffs the annual display of spring flowers has begun. Beside the cliff path, and in the more overgrown hedges, red campion is already in bloom. This will become more and more luxuriant as spring develops, the flowers varying from pale pink the deep rose red. In Guernsey French it is *violette d'fossai* – hedge campion – but in Guernsey English it goes by the far less attractive name of soldiers' fleas. I don't know what the unfortunate plant has done to deserve this name, unless it is that the flowers sometimes suffer from a smut disease which produces black spores.

Campions have male and female flowers on separate plants. The smut fungus, whose name is *Ustilago violacea*, attacks the female flowers. Normally the anthers of these flowers are rudimentary and do not develop, but the fungus causes them to grow and instead of pollen, fungal spores are produced inside them, turning them black.

Sweet Violets

In overgrown hedges, and in short turf beside the cliff paths, dog violets are beginning to flower. Sweet violets, with larger, rounded leaves and flowers of a deeper purple, have been in bloom all the winter, but they have finished flowering and now it is the turn of the dog violets. These have small, spade-shaped leaves, and flowers of a pale violet colour.

Both violets are native plants, but the sweet violet, with its sweetly scented flowers, has been cultivated in gardens for many centuries. It also used to be grown commercially for export. I remember how a corner of one of our fields used to be planted with rows of a large variety of sweet violet. The elderly couple who had planted them would keep the weeds down by hoeing between the rows, and in January and February they would pick and bunch the flowers and send them to Covent Garden.

Sweet violets still grow on roadside banks, and some may be descended from wild stock. But as they are often near houses, most have probably escaped from cultivation.

The dog violet has never been cultivated but this does not prevent it from invading gardens and establishing itself in paths and between stones, where its wiry roots are extremely difficult to eradicate. But it is attractive and harmless, and does not deserve its dog epithet. This was used in the middle ages to imply that it was in some way inferior, presumably because it had no scent.

A p r i l

We are enjoying a spell of the crystal-fine weather that sometimes comes our way in early spring. Recent rain has washed the dust from the air and sharpened the colours, and the sea, the cliffs and the lanes are almost painfully beautiful. From below, the bursting buds of the trees stand out against the blue sky, and in those elm trees that are still alive the bunches of dark stamens can be clearly seen projecting from the open flower buds. From the town the other islands look so close that you could touch them, and beyond them is the dark line of the French coast, with the menacing white scar of the nuclear reprocessing plant at Cap de la Hague.

In the garden the later varieties of daffodil are flowering, and the pear tree is covered (not just metaphorically, but literally) with white blossom. Soon it will be the turn of the apples and plums.

Above left: Pear blossom; above right: Apple blossom

At this time of year it would be difficult to imagine what the island would be like without alexanders, for the tall, handsome umbellifer has become an essential part of the landscape in early spring. The smooth, shining stems grow to a height of three or four feet, bearing glossy, light green leaves with rounded segments, and flattened leaf bases which sheath the stem. The plant is topped by numerous rounded heads of powdery, yellow-green flowers.

Alexanders are well suited to growing in woods and hedges, for the leaves and flowers are active early in the year, before they are shaded by the trees' leaves. But the plant is equally at home in full sunlight, and flourishes on the coastal headlands and dunes, and beside the cliff paths. At this time of the year most of the country lanes are lined with it – there are few parts of the island where none can be seen.

Despite its abundance, alexanders is not a native plant. It comes from the Mediterranean, and its name in medieval Latin was *Petroselinum Alexandrinum* – parsley of Alexandria. It may have been introduced into Britain by the Romans, or possibly by

Alexanders, a Mediterranean plant which has made itself at home.

the monks of the middle ages, for it is often found growing near old abbeys and monasteries. It was earthed-up and blanched like celery, and the flower heads were picked and eaten like cauliflower. In England it is never far from the sea, for it does not like heavy frosts. In Guernsey nowhere is too far from the sea for it to flourish.

In some years the alexanders are attacked by a rust disease, which covers the stems and leaves with spots of bright orange. The name of the fungus, which confines itself to alexanders, is *Puccinia smyrnii.*

In the summer the alexanders die down and are replaced by the equally abundant hogweed or cow-parsnip. I have noticed that for some reason cows, which love hogweed, do not touch alexanders, while horses are addicted to alexanders and will not eat hogweed. In the days of my youth I was allowed to exercise an elderly mare, and I used to ride her along the cliff paths near Le Gouffre (it would be illegal today.) Whenever we came to a clump of alexanders we had to stop, and I could not get her to move until she had finished the lot.

Kestrels are breeding in a ventilation hole high in the gable of the barn. They find the whole process immensely exciting. Since the birds of prey are at the top of the food chain there is no need for them to keep a low profile; on the contrary they are extremely noisy and visible. In the fields they screech as they chase each other from tree to tree, and their most intimate acts are performed on the ridge of the roof.

Opposite the hole is a tall cypress tree in which the cock-bird sits while his wife is laying. When he feels she has been sitting for long enough he goes off to catch a vole or a wood-mouse, and comes gliding down the field with the prey in his talons. Then he calls from the tree, and presents the mouse to the hen when she emerges.

Birds of prey regurgitate pellets containing the fur, feathers and bones they have been unable to digest. It is an interesting exercise to tease one of these out to see what they have been eating. In the case of our kestrels, the pellets which accumulate beneath the nest consist mainly of the blue-green wing cases of dung beetles. Kestrels are supposed to live mainly on small mammals, but it appears that the staple diet of our pair is beetles. Perhaps the daily mouse or vole which the cock presents to the hen has a ritual rather than a practical purpose.

Kestrels are by far the commonest birds of prey in Guernsey, both inland and on the coast. They can often be seen hovering over the cliffs, taking advantage of the up-current as the wind comes off the sea, and then folding their wings and dropping like a stone onto a mouse or insect they have seen moving below. They make no nest, but lay their eggs on a cliff ledge; inland they breed in abandoned crows' nests in the tree-tops, on ledges in quarry faces, or in holes in old buildings. As far as the kestrels are concerned there is no difference between a quarry face and an old building.

Kestrels are sometimes confused with sparrow-hawks, which are again breeding in Guernsey after an absence of about forty years. The birds are similar in size, but are easily distinguished by the shape of the wing and method of hunting. Kestrels hover, and have narrow, pointed wings. Sparrow-hawks have broad, rounded wings and do not hover, but patrol the hedges, darting from side to side in search of small (and not so small) birds. They can deal with anything up to the size of a pigeon, and have the unfortunate habit of raiding gardens and picking birds off bird-tables.

Sparrow-hawks breed in woodland and so far they are confined to the few areas of the island that are well wooded. They are never likely to be as common as kestrels, which are equally at home in fields, gardens, on the coastal commons or on the cliffs.

Sparrow-hawks are sometimes accused of causing a serious

decline in the numbers of small birds. More often it is magpies that get the blame. It is a common sight to see a pair of magpies patrolling a hedge or a garden in search of birds' nests, and sometimes they are caught red-handed with a nestling or an egg. And it is distressing to set up a bird table to encourage small birds into the garden, only to have them picked off by a sparrow-hawk. There is no doubt that there are fewer small birds than there used to be, while larger birds like magpies, crows, pigeons and herring gulls are on the increase. But the cause of the decline in small birds is not as simple as that. Cats, pesticides and slug pellets are at least as guilty.

The birds which have increased in number are the scavengers, and the reason they have increased is that we provide them with plenty to scavenge. Dead hedgehogs and blackbirds left on the roads by traffic, partially eaten takeaway meals and refuse sacks that they can easily open provide the magpies, crows and gulls with such a plentiful supply of food that they can successfully rear well over two young a year, and the population rises accordingly. The stolen nestlings are merely an *hors d'oeuvre*. If the magpies had to rely on their natural carrion and the occasional nestling, the population would be so small that they would have little impact on the small birds.

Three-cornered garlic is in bloom all over the island. The bell-shaped flower has six white petals, each with a green line down the centre. The flowers are grouped in an umbel, at the end of a stem which has three distinct corners. This distinguishes the plant from the other members of the onion family, whose flowering stems are round in section.

This difference does not prevent the plant from smelling powerfully of onions – indeed, it is almost always referred to in Guernsey as stinking onions. Cattle love it, and make straight for it when they are first turned out in the spring. Unfortunately

*Three-cornered garlic, an intro-
duction from the Mediterranean.*

the aromatic oil passes into the
milk. The taste may not be very
strong at the time, but you
notice it afterwards. I remember
when we used to keep cows the
family would complain that the
milk was undrinkable as long as
any garlic leaves remained in
the fields.

Like alexanders, three-
cornered garlic is an immigrant
from the Mediterranean which
has found a congenial home in
Guernsey. But while alexanders was introduced many centuries
ago as a pot herb, three-cornered garlic was brought in by
nineteenth century gardeners, who grew it for its ornamental
flowers. It flourished here and in the milder parts of Britain,
and soon escaped into the wild. It was first noticed in hedges in
Guernsey in 1847: the first record of the plant growing wild in
the British Isles. Since then it has become an abundant roadside
plant, both here and along the south coast of England.

It spreads efficiently – perhaps too efficiently – both by seed
and by division of the bulbs. Today it is in practically every hedge
in the island, often forming a band of white along the base of the
hedge, with the pink of the red campions above.

In Cornwall, where it also grows along the bases of the hedges,
three-cornered garlic is known as 'white bluebells'. It often
invades hedges where there are bluebells, and the two plants
make an attractive combination. But there is concern in Cornwall
that the bluebells do not seem to be able to compete with the
garlic, and die out as the garlic spreads. The two plants grow
together in some Guernsey hedges, for instance beside the road

in the Talbot Valley, but here there is no evidence that the bluebells are dying out.

Bluebells or wild hyacinths, unlike stinking onions, are truly native, and would have been growing in the oak forest which covered much of Guernsey when the first Neolithic settlers arrived. It is a plant with a very limited world distribution, being confined to the British Isles, the Low Countries and parts of France. It is normally thought of as a woodland plant, and in Guernsey it flourishes beneath the undergrowth in the wooded inland valleys. But it also grows in the open on the cliffs, shaded by the bracken with which it nearly always grows.

The most spectacular display is in the Bluebell Woods, on the cliff slopes between Fort George and Fermain. Here, the bulbs are shaded mainly by sycamore, and the undergrowth of bramble has been cleared to give an uninterrupted view of acres of bluebells. It is so spectacular that many people make an annual pilgrimage to the Bluebell Woods, to walk the paths which wind between the sheets of blue, whose intensity comes as a fresh surprise each year.

The bluebells are in flower now, before the bracken fronds have grown high enough to hide the flowers from the pollinating insects. The season is all too short: soon the flowers will be replaced by seed capsules and the leaves will rot, their substance to be returned to the bulbs, which will spend the summer lying dormant under the canopy of bracken.

In the autumn, when the bracken fronds die they will

Bluebells, a native flower

quickly break down to produce a thick layer of humus, protecting and nourishing the bluebell bulbs, which will already have grown new leaves and flower buds. Then in early spring the flowering stems will shoot up, the cliff slopes and the valley terraces will shimmer with violet-blue, and the annual pilgrimage will again be made to the Bluebell Woods.

Where have all the swallows gone? And, come to think of it, the house-martins and swifts? My thoughts turned in this direction the other day, on a visit to Herm. Over the cliffs just south of the Rosière landing, a large mixed flock of swallows and house-martins were wheeling and diving, the martins flashing their white rumps as they twisted and turned below the cliff path.

How welcome these birds would be, if only they would stay with us to breed. But they were on migration from their winter quarters in Africa to their breeding grounds in Britain, the Low Countries or Scandinavia. They had obviously discovered a rich source of insects over the cliff slopes, and had interrupted their journey to re-fuel. Few if any of them will stop to breed locally.

There was a time when, from mid-April until October, the air above the fields would have been full of swallows and martins. Depending on where the midges were flying, the birds might be so high that you could hardly see them, or skimming the ground and weaving between tussocks of grass. There are still usually some to be seen over the coast, where the supply of insects seems to be particularly rich. Inland, at least in our part of the island, they have become a rare sight.

Large flocks of swallows and martins do not necessarily mean that we are about to enjoy a fine summer. The birds are no better at forecasting the weather than we are. They wait for a settled spell before beginning their migration, but they have no idea what conditions will be like when once they have embarked on their long journey. My large flock over Herm simply indicated that the birds have been lucky with the weather so far.

As far as house martins are concerned, disaster struck in 1991, when they encountered appalling weather on their journey north. Most never made it, and those that did reach us arrived too late to breed successfully. This interrupted their breeding pattern, traditional nest sites were forgotten, and the martins have never fully recovered. There are plenty of suitable breeding places waiting for them under the eaves of the all-too-numerous houses, but finding a suitable nesting site is only one of their problems. We have no control over what happens to them in Africa (indeed we do not even know exactly where they spend the winter). Nor can we help them on their hazardous twice-yearly migration.

Swallows are also declining, and here the problem probably is a lack of nesting sites. They like to build their nests of mud among the rafters of old barns and outhouses – a category of building which is becoming scarce as more and more are converted into human abodes.

Swifts do not seem to have been affected to the same extent. They are much larger and stronger than swallows and martins, and they travel later in the spring. Two hundred years ago Gilbert White noted that in hard springs they did not arrive in his Hampshire parish until the beginning of May, and that is still the case today. In the autumn they leave long before the other birds, usually in the first week of August.

During the three months of their stay in Guernsey we can usually see a few swifts if we gaze long enough into the sky. I don't know where they are breeding – there are very few buildings near here that are tall enough to suit them. They are a commoner sight over the town, where they breed under the pantiles of some of the tallest town houses, as well as in church steeples.

M a y

The spring migration continues. Soon most of the birds which use the island as a staging post will have passed through, and will be occupying their northern breeding grounds. A small proportion will have decided to go no further, and will spend the summer with us. Some of these will be young, non-breeding birds. Others will breed here.

While it is common to see birds of passage feeding and resting at this time of year, it is much more difficult to see the actual migration. One of the best places to see migration in progress is Lihou Island. Although joined to Guernsey at low tide by a causeway, Lihou has a wild and remote atmosphere, and is ideally placed on the birds' migration route along the western coastal fringe of Europe.

Depending on weather conditions an amazing range of

Above: Fulmar, a welcome recent arrival.

migrants can be seen feeding on the shore, darting among the bracken or resting in the lee of the drystone walls.

After years of being a private island Lihou now belongs to the States of Guernsey. The day on which States members were invited to view their new acquisition, in the spring of 1995, was perfectly timed, for the island was swarming with birds. Blackcap, pied flycatcher, cuckoo, whitethroat, swallows, wheatears and sedge warblers were there in spectacular numbers. Even the walled garden around the house was alive with birds. Let us hope that the States are not tempted to develop the island as a 'heritage centre' or any other kind of centre; it would be all too easy to destroy Lihou's unique atmosphere. It would also deprive the wildlife, and the people who visit it for a few hours at low spring tides, of one of the few remaining remote spots in the Channel Islands.

One of the last of our summer visitors to arrive is – or perhaps I should say was – the spotted flycatcher. A pair of these charming little birds used to breed each year in the creeper against the barn wall. They would arrive from southern Africa in early May and sit on the electric fence which surrounds the field, watching for flying insects. When one saw a fly or gnat it would dart after it, there would be an audible snap of the beak, and the bird would return to precisely the same spot on the wire to watch for the next victim.

The female would build an intricate cup-shaped nest of mosses, lichens and cobwebs between the creeper and the wall, and lay five or six pale, mottled eggs. Throughout the summer the parents would work all day to feed their clamouring family, and in September they would return to Africa.

In the spring of 1992 the flycatchers failed to return. Ours were not the only ones – some catastrophe struck the whole population, either in Africa or on migration, and they arrived in Europe either late or not at all. They have not yet fully recovered. We still see the occasional spotted flycatcher hawking from the wire in spring and autumn, but they have never again stayed with us to breed.

Most of the numerous waders which spend the winter on our shoreline will by now have flown north to their breeding grounds in northern Britain, Scandinavia and the Arctic tundra. Apart from the ringed plover, which breeds in very small numbers on one or two of our beaches, the only wader to stay all the year round and breed here regularly is the oystercatcher. We shall return to this striking, noisy and altogether splendid bird in October.

The wild orchids are beginning to bloom. Already the low-lying meadows near the west coast are tinged with magenta, and by the middle of the month they will be blazing with colour. Besides several species of orchid, there are Lady's smock, ragged robin, meadow buttercup and galingale, with sweet vernal grass in the drier places and yellow flag irises in the ditches.

Unimproved meadowland is a habitat which is becoming rare all over Europe, and Guernsey is no exception. Not long ago all the meadows inland from the coast in the lower parts of the island, and the floors of most of the inland valleys, were fully used for grazing and hay-making. The water table was never far from the surface, and the meadows were often under water in winter. In the spring the ground was still too wet to allow cattle to graze without destroying the turf, so the hay was allowed to grow until the late summer, when it was mown, dried and stored for the winter. This allowed plenty of time for the orchids and other flowers to finish flowering and set seed.

By August the upland fields were so dry that the grass was no longer growing, and the cattle were running short of grazing. But the meadow soil was still damp, and the grass began to grow as soon as the hay had been carted. This was the aftermath: an entirely beneficial thing, without the slightly sinister connotations that the word has acquired today.

The meadows were grazed through the autumn, until the soil

became too wet to support the cattle without breaking through the turf. Then they were left to the snipe and the curlews until hay-making time came round again.

Because they could not be used in the winter, some landowners regarded the low-lying meadows as their least valuable land, and many were used as building sites for houses and vineries. Of those that remain, most have been 'improved' by drainage schemes to lower the water table, and by ploughing, fertilizing and re-seeding. From the point of view of an intensive farmer this makes sense, but from the point of view of wildlife it is a disaster. The meadows have an immensely rich and varied flora, and the plants in turn support a wide variety of animals. When 'improved' the field becomes an almost pure stand of perennial ryegrass, and the meadow community is destroyed.

In order to protect some of the remaining meadowland, La Société Guernesiaise has bought several meadows in La Rue des Vicheries, St. Peter's, just inland from Rocquaine Bay. By managing them in the traditional way they have not only preserved the orchids and other flowers, but increased their numbers.

The most spectacular flower, by far, is *Orchis laxiflora*. There is no mistaking this beautiful orchid, for the clear magenta flowers are well spaced out on a long stem, which stands two feet or more high. It does not grow in the United Kingdom, and many English flower books ignore it. Those that do mention it, call it the Jersey orchid. It used to be quite common in that island, but building in Beaumont Marsh destroyed one of its best habitats, the proliferation of golf courses destroyed others, and now it is even rarer in Jersey than it is in Guernsey. Perhaps a better name is the loose-flowered orchid, a direct translation of its Latin name.

Growing among them are a scattering of southern marsh orchids. These have a dense pyramidal head of flowers, of a pinker shade than the loose-flowered orchids. There are also two species with spotted leaves – common and heath spotted orchids

Loose-flowered orchid, a Channel Islands speciality

– and every gradation of hybrid between them.

The orchid meadows are well worth a visit in May. If you drive there, leave the car in a coastal car park and walk inland where there is a postbox in a green traffic island, just north of the old fish factory. When you reach an electricity sub-station in the hedge ahead of you, one meadow is behind it, and the others are down the lane to the left.

In order to maintain a sufficiently high water table, it is necessary to have control of the drainage over as wide an area as possible, and the Société is building up a fund to buy more meadows as they become available.

In the Talbot Valley the National Trust of Guernsey has succeeded in bringing orchids back to one of the meadows in the floor of the valley. This, too, is worth a visit. As well as loose-flowered orchids there are numerous southern marsh orchids, and a rich selection of other meadow flowers. The meadow is on the south side of the road, just west of the lane to Les Niaux mill. The entrance is marked by a National Trust stone.

Loose-flowered orchids may not grow in the UK but they are widespread in Europe, North Africa and West Asia, and could not be described as an endangered species in world-wide terms. What is endangered is the meadow habitat. Moreover, Guernsey's meadows are unique, for nowhere else will the same collection of plants and animals be found living together.

Futhermore the 'hybrid swarm' of intermediate stages between the various orchid species is of botanical importance. But above all the meadows are beautiful.

The fulmars have been occupying their precarious breeding ledges on the cliffs since February, and by now each hen will have laid her single egg and the pair will be taking turns to incubate it. On a visit to Herm the other day we counted seven of the large, white birds on their nests in the most precipitous and inaccessible parts of the cliffs between Putrainez and Caquorobert, while their mates flew busily around, paying frequent visits to the nests.

Fulmars are large petrels. They are true seabirds, spending most of their lives at sea and feeding by skimming the surface for plankton and anything else they can find. They have benefited from the extremely wasteful methods of industrial fishing. Everything is scooped up by the trawlers but about 40% of the catch is thrown back, where it floats, dead, on the surface, to be picked up by gannets, fulmars and gulls.

Until the end of the last century the only place where fulmars bred in the British Isles was the remote island group of St. Kilda, far out to the west of the Outer Hebrides. They bred in enormous numbers and were an important source of food for the St. Kildans, who would scale the immense cliffs to snare the birds.

Early in the present century the fulmars began to extend their range southwards, reaching Cornwall in 1939. After the war they began to be seen off the Channel Islands. In 1974 the first fulmar was seen ashore, on the north cliffs of Jersey, among a colony of razorbills. The following year several pairs attempted to breed, and at least one chick was raised. In 1975 they also bred for the first time in Alderney, on the cliffs opposite the main gannet colony on the Garden Rocks. During the 1980s the fulmars established breeding colonies in Guernsey, Sark, Herm and Jethou, and they have since extended into Brittany.

The best place to see fulmars in Guernsey is the stretch of cliff to the west of Les Tielles, particularly around Le Long Cavaleux and Belle Elizabeth. Superficially the fulmars resemble the herring gulls which are usually wheeling round the cliffs with them, but they are easily distinguished from gulls by their cigar-shaped bodies, and by their rapid, stiff-winged flight. Gulls have a leisurely wing-beat in which the middle of the wing starts to rise while the tip is still falling. Fulmars' wings are set well back on the body, and beat more rapidly, or are held out stiffly as the bird glides. When at sea they have no fear of the wildest storm, skimming between the waves and often banking so steeply that the wings are vertical, with one wing-tip appearing to touch the water. I still associate fulmars with the Hebrides and the deep ocean, and find it immensely satisfying that they are now breeding in these islands.

❂

The garden is at its most colourful at this time of year. The daffodils are over, and it will be another month before their leaves have died down and I can cut the grass where they are naturalised. But the lilac and wisteria are blooming in their full glory, the first rose buds are opening, and self-sown forget-me-nots are covering the flower beds with a pale blue haze. The forget-me-nots are a mixed blessing, for they seed themselves prolifically and smother everything else if given the chance. They are beautiful at the moment, but when they have finished flowering we will remove most of the plants, leaving just a few to set seed and provide for the next generation.

Normally at this time of year the most eye-catching feature of the garden is the vivid magenta of the Madeiran cranesbill, *Geranium maderense*. This year there are no flowers, as all the mature plants perished in the frosts of January. Numerous seedlings from previous years are germinating, however. Given two mild winters they will flower in two years' time. Another striking exotic, the giant echium or rocket plant, is slightly hardier and survived all over the garden, for this is another free-seeder. Already the first mauve flowers have opened and are attracting numerous bumble-bees.

In a reckless moment during the winter, when May seemed a long way off, I offered to open the garden to a local gardening group. A day was chosen in the early part of the month, when the display should have been at its best. The night before the visit there was a gale which brought branches down from the trees, and capsized many of the giant echiums. In the morning there was a cloudburst which flattened the herbaceous plants. By the afternoon the sun was shining, but the visitors had to pick their way between sodden, straggling plants and drunkenly leaning echiums. It was very different from a National Trust garden, but most of them seemed to enjoy it.

For the last few days a cuckoo has been calling intermittently from the trees at the top of the field. There is no more evocative sound of early summer, and the bird is most welcome, even if it does have anti-social habits when it comes to breeding.

Cuckoo, welcome in spite of its anti-social habits

The first cuckoos arrive each year in mid-April. It has become something of a competition to be the first to write to the local paper claiming to have heard it. Since the collared dove arrived in Guernsey the reports of cuckoos have been getting earlier and earlier; it is sometimes claimed in February or even January. The collared dove does sometimes sound like a cuckoo, but when you hear the clear, liquid notes of the real thing there is no mistaking it.

In early summer years ago the cuckoo would often call all day, and well into the night. I remember it particularly on wet, still days, when the sound would carry among the dripping trees. Today we are lucky if we hear it calling for a few minutes on one or two days in May and June, though there is a better chance of hearing it in the wilder coastal areas such as Herm Common. Nobody knows exactly why cuckoo numbers have dropped. The almost universal use of pesticides and a shortage of foster-birds' nests must be part of the reason.

Adult cuckoos feed on caterpillars, particularly the hairy ones which no other bird can deal with. The young are fed on whatever the foster-parents would give their own young. One possible reason why cuckoos entrust their young to another species to rear is that hairy caterpillars are not a suitable diet for young cuckoos. Foster parents include robins, warblers and pipits. Perhaps the reason cuckoos favour coastal heaths and commons is the number of nests of meadow and rock pipits to be found there.

Having no parental duties to detain them, the adult cuckoos leave for their 'winter' quarters in Africa in July – the first migratory birds to leave. When once they are independent from their long-suffering foster parents, the young cuckoos switch to a diet of caterpillars, and build up a supply of fat to sustain them on their long journey. Finally, in August or September, they too depart for Africa. How do young cuckoos, travelling independently, without their parents, find their way to their ancestral homes in central and southern Africa, when they have never made the journey before? That is one of the many unsolved riddles of nature.

At about the same time as the cuckoo is calling, many of the plants in the garden, in the hedges and on the cliffs become covered with 'cuckoo-spit'. In our garden at present there are white flecks of foam on a variety of plants, particularly lavender and honeysuckle.

Despite their name, the only connection between 'cuckoo-spit' and the cuckoo is that both appear at the same time of the year. The white froth is in fact protecting the young stage of a small plant-sucking bug. Because of its squat appearance, and ability to leap, it is called a frog-hopper.

The adult is a brownish insect about a quarter of an inch long. In the autumn it lays its eggs on plant stems, where they lie dormant during the winter. In the spring the egg hatches and the young insect, or nymph, climbs until it reaches a young, tender shoot, pierces it with its needle-like jaws and feeds on the sap. It now surrounds itself with spume, made from a liquid secreted in the abdomen and blown into bubbles by bellows built into the sides of the body. The spume provides some protection against predators, although it is no defence against one species of solitary wasp, which drags the nymphs from their spume and uses them to stock a larder to provide for its own larvae when they hatch. More importantly, the spume protects the delicate nymph from drying up. It even contains a substance which prevents the bubbles from dissolving in wet weather.

Inside their envelopes of spume the nymphs are feeding and growing, changing as they do so from white to green, and finally to brown. Soon the first adult frog-hoppers, complete with wings, will extract themselves from the froth. Most will mature in June, although some 'cuckoo-spit' will continue to appear on the plants throughout the summer.

J u n e

Hedge-cutting time is here again. It is up to the owners of all the hedges bordering public roads and footpaths to make sure that they are trimmed twice a year to the satisfaction of the parish authorities. The first inspection will be in a fortnight's time. All over the island the lanes are being blocked by tractors and machinery, and one by one the hedgebanks are emerging from the vegetation like shorn lambs.

Inevitably some wild flowers will be cut down in the process, and from time to time letters appear in the paper deploring this. But April and May are the months when the hedges are at their most floriferous. By the beginning of June most of the flowers have died down, and the hedges have assumed a distinctly scruffy appearance. The purpose of the twice-yearly trim is to prevent the roads from becoming blocked by vegetation, but it is

Above: Long-eared bat

52

also to the wild flowers' advantage. Without it the campions, violets and primroses would quickly be smothered by coarse grasses, hogweed and brambles. It is the hedge-cutting in June and September that enables the hedges to produce the early spring display for which Guernsey is famous.

While today the inspection of the hedges is carried out in a dignified and unostentatious manner by the parish Douzaines, to our medieval ancestors it was an excuse for a jollification. *La Chevauchée de St. Michel* was one of the most colourful and elaborate feudal ceremonies in the British Isles. The feudal court of St. Michel had the responsibility of seeing that the roads were maintained, and every three years an inspection was made. The cavalcade consisted of mounted dignitaries and footmen, or *pions*. There were various stopping places where feudal dues were paid in kind. *La Table des Pions* at Pleinmont is where breakfast was served to the *pions*. There was no shortage of *pions*, for they were allowed to kiss any girl they could catch.

One of the court officials carried a long wand, and if this was obstructed by encroaching vegetation, the owner of the property was fined on the spot. The day's takings went towards a good dinner when the work was done.

La Chevauchée, together with most of the other medieval customs, did not find favour with the Puritans and was suppressed at the Reformation. It has been revived occasionally in modern times. It was performed in 1966 to mark the ninth centenary of the Battle of Hastings, when Guernsey (helped by the rest of Normandy) conquered England, and again in 1995 when it was revived by the National Trust of Guernsey, fifty years after the Liberation.

For the farmer who still makes hay, the June hedge-cutting comes at the busiest time of the year. Grass which is to be preserved as silage can be harvested earlier in the year, but the first half of June is the best time for hay-making. Before then it is difficult to get it dry, and if it is left much later the grass will put all its energy into seeding, and much of the food value will

Hogweed, a proscribed 'noxious weed'

be lost. Of course, everything depends on the weather. There is no point in mowing the hay unless sunny weather is likely for the next few days. If it is not, the farmer can get on with his hedges.

He can also tackle his 'noxious weeds'. The law decrees that nettles, ragwort, hogweed, docks of all kinds, thistles and hemlock water-dropwort must be destroyed before they come into flower or seed. Anyone who permits these plants to set seed on his land is guilty of an offence under the Noxious Weeds (Guernsey) Law of 1952. The law is still in force, although few people take much notice of it. If you allow your hedge to encroach into the road you soon hear about it. But if you allow ragwort to flower and blow its seeds around the island nothing is said. Perhaps it is time for the Noxious Weeds Law, which dates from a time when agriculture and horticulture were major industries, to be either scrapped or updated. Certainly the list of proscribed weeds could be shortened. Nettles are an important food plant for the larvae of many insects, including some of the most beautiful butterflies, and they tend to grow only on marginal land. In fields they are automatically controlled by normal cultivation. Hogweed or cow-parsnip grows everywhere, and its umbels of white flowers are part of the early summer scene. On grazing land it is no problem, for cattle love it. The sap does cause a rash in some people if it comes into contact with the skin, but not to the same extent as giant hogweed, or cartwheel plant, which is positively dangerous. Fortunately giant hogweed does not grow in Guernsey, except in one or two gardens where it must have been deliberately planted.

Docks are annoying weeds of pasture, but stay where they are and affect only the farmer who allows them to grow. Thistles are more of a public nuisance, as the parachute seeds blow into everybody else's land. By far the most serious weed is ragwort. This also has parachute seeds, and appears in fields, on the coast and even in town gardens. In appearance it is like a large groundsel, with crinkly leaves and heads of golden yellow flowers. It does not mind drought, and after a long, dry summer it is often the only green plant in a field. It is an attractive wild flower – but it is deadly to cattle and horses. They dislike the taste and smell, and will leave it alone when grazing but in silage they are unable to sort it from the grass. The poison it contains is not destroyed by drying, and in hay it is equally poisonous. Worst of all, if it is killed by spraying with herbicide it becomes palatable and may be eaten by grazing animals, but is still just as poisonous.

Hemlock water-dropwort, a celery-like weed of wet places, is also poisonous. The swollen roots, looking rather like dahlia tubers, are deadly. Cattle are sometimes killed when the roots are exposed during the cleaning of water-courses, and there have been several cases of people being poisoned after mistaking them for parsnips.

Personally I would keep ragwort, hemlock water-dropwort and possibly thistles on the list of 'noxious weeds', and forget about the rest.

Haymaking is bad news for small mammals, particularly voles, which make their runs among the grass stems at ground level. When the hay is being mown, one or other of our resident pair of kestrels sits on a branch as close to the tractor as possible and swoops down if a vole is exposed to view.

The Guernsey vole is one of the few animals – perhaps the only one – peculiar to the island of Guernsey. It is quite large, with a short tail, blunt snout, small ears and a fat, sausage-shaped body. Opinions differ over whether it should be named as a distinct species, or merely a variety of the continental short-tailed field vole. Whichever is the case, it has been isolated in Guernsey long enough to develop characteristics which distinguish it from any other vole.

The Jersey vole is quite different: it is a bank vole, similar to that found in England, but larger. At the opposite end of the British Isles, the Orkney archipelago has a short-tailed field vole very similar to the Guernsey vole, and yet there is no related vole on the British mainland.

The other small mammals of the Channel Islands have an equally complicated geographical distribution. It is usually explained by suggesting that the animals invaded the area in waves after the Ice Age. Guernsey has deep water between it and the Continent, and has been an island longer than either Jersey or England. Any animal which managed to get here before Guernsey was isolated would not have to face competition from later arrivals, which could reach Jersey and England until comparatively recently.

In the case of the voles, the Orkney and Guernsey voles are probably the survivors of short-tailed field voles which once covered the whole of Britain, but were replaced later in mainland Britain and in Jersey by the bank vole. But it is not as simple as that, and nobody has yet produced a theory that adequately explains the distribution of the other animals, particularly the shrews.

Despite the hazards of hay making, we must still have a

thriving population of both voles and shrews, for they constitute a large part of the diet of the barn owls. The pellets which the owls spit out, and which accumulate beneath their nesting hole, are full of the skulls and bones of voles and shrews. The shrews are white-toothed, of a continental species which is not found in the United Kingdom.

Woodmouse, larger and paler than its English cousins.

The cats, too, enjoy catching both voles and shrews. A fat vole makes a good meal for a cat, but they obviously find the shrews distasteful, for they leave the little animals on the mat, for us to find and dispose of on the morning. They are tiny, mouse-like creatures with a long, pointed snout and ears almost hidden in the grey fur. They are not rodents but insectivores, with sharp teeth and an extremely high rate of metabolism, which makes it necessary for them to forage for food almost continuously. For this reason they cannot hibernate, but must continue their endless search for insects, worms and woodlice throughout the winter. They are harmless, even beneficial creatures, and it is distressing that the cats catch so many, apparently purely for sport.

The cats also bring in the occasional wood mouse, which they find in the hedges after dark. They are larger than house mice, with an extremely long tail. Sometimes the tail is the only part left on the mat. Again there are island differences: ours are slightly larger and paler than their English cousins, but the differences are very small and not enough to justify giving the Guernsey wood mouse a separate name.

Flowers, like small mammals, sometimes have a distribution which is difficult to explain. The southern cliffs of Herm are about the same height and have the same aspect as those of Guernsey, and conditions on them must be very similar. Yet there are some strange differences in the plants which grow on them.

Nottingham catchfly is unknown in Guernsey, yet in Herm it is plentiful. Joshua Gosselin, the author of a list of plants which was in effect the first *Flora* of Guernsey, found it in Herm in about 1758. His specimen survives. It is labelled: 'in the island of Erm.' The catchfly is still there. Walking along the cliff path the other day we passed several clumps, growing on the landward side of the path to the west of Putrainez. They were not unlike sea campions, but more weedy and straggling, with drooping flowers. Since it was daytime the petals were curled inwards and the flowers appeared to be dead. If we could have returned at dusk the deeply notched, light cream petals would have been open, and there would have been a strong scent.

The flowers have an elaborate mechanism which ensures cross-pollination. The stem has a sticky zone just below the flowers, which prevents ants from climbing into the flowers and stealing the pollen and nectar, without pollinating the flowers. The scent and light-coloured petals attract night-flying moths. There are ten stamens, and each flower opens on three successive nights.

On the first night five stamens ripen and are extended; the

second night the other five are extended, so that any visiting moth will be dusted with pollen. By the third night all the stamens will have died back but the stigmas, which collect pollen, will be extended. So any pollen they receive must come from another flower in an earlier stage of development.

Nottingham catchfly is so called because it was first found on the walls of Nottingham Castle. There is a tenuous Guernsey connection : William Willisel, the botanist who found it in 1670, had been head gardener to Sir John Lambert, the Cromwellian general, who after the Civil War was imprisoned in Castle Cornet. Lambert was a keen gardener, and the small garden he is thought to have created in the castle has recently been restored and stocked with plants which he might have grown. He is known to have cultivated the Guernsey lily in his London garden, and doubtless grew it also at Castle Cornet.

Nottingham Catchfly no longer grows at Nottingham Castle, or indeed anywhere else in Nottinghamshire, but it still grows on a few dry banks, cliffs and shingle beaches in other parts of the country – and in Herm.

It is the longest day of the year. The birds are taking advantage of the long hours of daylight by foraging for their young families almost round the clock. As we go to bed the blackbirds are still groping their way about the lawn after worms, and long before we wake they are back at work. For migratory birds one of the main advantages of flying to northern latitudes to breed is the length of the northern summer day. It is equally useful for our resident robins and blue tits. The tits have a large family in a hole in the wall of the house, and keep up a continuous shuttle service between it and the vegetable garden, where they seem to find an unlimited supply of insects. I dread to think what the insects would do to the garden plants if it were not for the blue tits.

I don't know where the robins are nesting. It must be

somewhere close to the lawn, for whenever one of the cats settles down, hoping for a quiet snooze in the sun, it is scolded by an angry robin, bobbing up and down on a branch just out of the cat's reach. The furious scolding continues until the cat can stand it no longer and stalks away, its tail twitching in embarrassment.

To the barn owls, feeding a growing family inside a ventilation hole above our bedroom, midsummer is a difficult time, the short nights barely giving them time to stock the larder. At the end of a long day they are forced to start hunting while it is still light. About half an hour before dusk, after sitting at the entrance to the hole and surveying the landscape for a few minutes, they fly silently into the fields and patrol the hedges for voles, shrews and wood mice.

Bats have the same problem. They need plenty of insects to keep them going, and have very little time in which to catch them. They emerge from their daytime hiding places before it is dark, and begin hawking backwards and forwards among the trees.

Bat numbers have declined everywhere in recent years, partly because of insecticides, but mainly because of the destruction of the old barns, ivy-covered tree stumps and generally derelict places where they like to hide during the daytime. The urge for tidiness is a purely human phenomenon, and needs to be resisted for the sake of all the other creatures, which suffer from our obsessive tidiness. A little untidiness would be far more beneficial to wildlife than all the international conventions, protocols, strategies and laws put together.

When the long days return and the bats are out at dusk, we are always delighted to see that our own untidiness has paid off, and the bats are back on their favourite beat between the house and the surrounding trees.

Bats are extremely difficult to identify on the wing. Both pipistrelles and long-eared bats are resident in Guernsey. Judging by their relatively large size ours are long-eared bats. I don't know where they hide during the day – there are plenty of ivy-covered trees for them to choose from – but during the night one of them has the habit of hanging from a rafter in the barn while it devours its catch. By the morning the bat has gone, leaving on the floor a pile of small, black droppings and not-so-small moth wings.

Fairly recently it has been recognised that there are two distinct species of long-eared bat: a brown British species and a grey continental one. Judging by the bodies which have been identified, most of the Channel Island long-eared bats are grey ones from the Continent.

The cabbage palm outside our front door is flowering. Projecting from each rosette of sword-shaped leaves at the top of the tree is a flowering stem. These appeared a few days ago and grew rapidly, branching to form twigs with flower buds arranged along them. One by one the small, white flowers are opening, and attracting crowds of bees. In the evening the heavy, sweet scent hangs on the air and drifts in through the windows.

The cabbage palm, *Cordyline australis*, is not a true palm tree but a member of the agave family. It comes from New Zealand and received its name because the first settlers thought it looked like a cabbage on a long stalk. It does not like hard frost, but is sufficiently hardy to grow along the south coast of England, and as far north as the west coast of Scotland.

It was brought to Guernsey early in the nineteenth century and has flourished here, being cut back only in the severest winters. The last occasion was in January 1987, when nearly every cabbage palm in the island lost its leaves and appeared to be dead. In most cases the trunks eventually rotted or were felled, but new shoots arose from the stumps, and now there are clumps of palms where before there were single trees.

Our tree was no exception. When it was obviously dead we felled it, and when sprouts arose from the roots we reduced them to a single shoot. This grew rapidly and flowered for the first time in 1995. After flowering it began to branch, and now it has several branches, each with a new flowering stem.

It has to be said that later in the summer the old leaves die, but remain hanging from the tree in a decidedly derelict manner. One of my regular August jobs is to get a ladder and pull off the long, immensely tough dead leaves. If this is not done they come down one by one during the winter, killing the lawn and obstructing the path.

Cabbage palms tend to figure rather frequently in tourist brochures, for they do give the place a semi-tropical appearance. It is just as well they were not all killed in 1987.

J u l y

The vegetable kingdom is winning. Normally by the beginning of July the soil is dry, plant growth has slowed down, and we can relax and enjoy the garden. The weather now is idyllic. Calm weather – really calm, without a breath of wind – is most unusual in the Channel Islands, yet for the last few days that is what we have been enjoying, together with cloudless skies. But June was unusually wet, and the combination or moist soil and warmth is causing the plants to run riot. The lawn is growing almost while you watch it, the vegetables are struggling up through the luxuriant weeds, and roses and shrubs are blocking the paths.

Sleeping beauty slept for a hundred years, and during that time the wicked fairy caused an impenetrable barrier of trees and briars to spring up around her palace. I would imagine that nature could easily cut that time to single figures. If we were to

Above: Honeysuckle and humming-bird hawk moth

stop gardening for three or four years, the tax man (or whoever was the first to notice that we were no longer in circulation) would have to hack his way through a jungle of tree saplings, shrub roses and giant echiums. If he left it for twenty years he would find a forest, mainly of ash and sycamore, with a dense undergrowth of briars and brambles.

The winged seeds of ash and sycamore get everywhere. They spring up in the lawn, the flower beds and paths, and even on the roof and in the gutters. If the seedlings are not ruthlessly dealt with in no time they are young trees. The oak takes longer to become established, but in the end it would see off all competition. If the tax man left it for a hundred years before bringing his bill, he would find an oak forest.

Fortunately things have not yet reached that stage, and we are managing to maintain some contact with the outside world. And it is nice to see the lawn looking green and healthy – normally by this stage in the summer it is worn and brown.

The lawn is by no means all grass. Presumably somebody once cleared the ground and sowed lawn grass, but that was a long time ago and over the years other plants have crept in and made themselves so much at home that now the original grasses would be hard to find. We have never used any herbicides, or any other sort of chemical for that matter; the only factor determining which plants can invade the lawn is the mowing machine. In spite of the mowing, a surprising number of unofficial plants manage to keep their heads down and flourish just out of reach of the machine. When I counted them not long ago I found thirty species living happily together.

The common lawn daisy, or course, is everywhere, opening its flowers in the morning in all but the worst weather, at any time of the year. They are beheaded by the mower, but by the following morning a fresh crop has opened. They can grow, not only from seed but from the smallest piece of stem or leaf, so the mowing machine ensures that they are spread more or less evenly over the lawn. John Gerard, the sixteenth century herbalist, was enthusiastic about the virtues of the daisy (but then he was enthusiastic about practically everything). 'The Daisies,' he said, 'do mitigate all kinde of paines, but especially in the joints, and gout, if they be stamped with new butter unsalted, and applied upon the pained place.'

Daisies, a cure for all ills

Gerard was even more enthusiastic about self-heal, another constituent of our lawn. This is a herb of the deadnettle family, with small, purple-violet flowers. In long vegetation it can grow to about a foot in height, but on the lawn it stays at ground level, and spreads sideways to form mats. The flowers are arranged in flat-topped heads which just manage to avoid the mowing machine. They began to appear as soon as midsummer was past, and now there are purple patches all over the lawn, attractive both to us and to the bees. Self-heal was used to cure wounds. Another name, both here and in England, was carpenter's herb, presumably because of its ability to cure chisel wounds. Gerard thought it was the best wound herb of all, and claimed that a decoction of self-heal with wine and water 'doth joine together and make whole and sound all wounds both inward and outward.' Moreover, when bruised with rose oil and vinegar and laid on the forehead, it could cure headache.

Other wild flowers on the lawn include dandelion, cat's-ear, white clover, thyme-leaved speedwell, primrose, yarrow and, on one occasion, Lady's tresses. We were delighted when this tiny white orchid appeared, apparently from nowhere, but it disappeared as mysteriously as it had come.

A plant which would cheerfully take over the garden if given the chance is *Solierolia solierolii*, more usually known as mind-your-own-business. It is a creeping plant with thread-like stems and tiny, rounded leaves, which forms a green blanket along the edges of paths and at the bases of walls. It covers the soil at the edge of the lawn, and invades the lawn in places where the grass is not vigorous enough to smother it. It is a flowering plant, although the reddish-brown flowers are so minute that you need a magnifying glass to see them.

Mind-your-own-business is a native of Corsica, Sardinia and the Balearic Islands. It must have been in Guernsey for a long time, for it is well established around most of the old houses. It does not like frost, and is cut back by the occasional hard winter, but enough always survives in cracks in the masonry to recolonise the garden. In moderation it is an attractive plant, and a good way of covering the ground where nothing else will grow. But when it invades the flower beds and smothers the flowers, it has to be dealt with severely.

The blackbirds have managed to raise a third brood this year. They have been nesting in the ivy covering a low wall beside the lawn. Now young birds seem to be everywhere, hopping after their parents and begging for worms. We are pleased to see them as we suspected that the first brood was taken by magpies.

Normally by this time of the year the dry surface soil has forced the earthworms to retreat to deeper layers, where they curl up and wait for the rains to return. The blackbirds then switch their attention to the soft fruit. They enjoy the raspberries and currants but it is not a suitable diet for nestlings, so the blackbirds do not attempt to breed again.

This July the worms are still at the surface, and the parents are teaching their third family of the year how to catch them. This means that we have been allowed to harvest our own raspberries and blackcurrants, though the birds still had most of their favourite redcurrants. For some reason they have also developed a taste for gooseberries. This surprises me, for normally these are too acid even for the blackbirds.

There is also a family of thrushes in the garden. This is particularly pleasing, for these birds seem to have declined in numbers in the last few years, and last year we rarely saw one. Apart from the pleasure of seeing and hearing the birds, they are welcome as they are expert at dealing with snails. There are plenty of holes and crannies in the walls where garden snails can hide, and at night they come out and devour the plants. But they have to contend with hedgehogs at night and thrushes by day, and between them these keep the snail population within reasonable bounds.

The thrushes in the garden are song thrushes. The larger, paler and more upright mistle thrushes prefer the fields, where there is more space around them, though they sometimes venture into the garden when the myrtle berries are ripe. They, too, have had a good year; the fields seem to have provided plenty of worms for them, as well as dung beetles for the crows and kestrels.

The crows have raised a family of three in their untidy pile of sticks at the extreme summit of an oak tree overhanging the garden. The parent birds enjoy hanging on to the topmost branches as they sway in the wind, but now that the children are as large as their parents, the family spend most of the day pottering around in the field. The five crows are usually in a tight group, as if conferring over some important matter.

The kestrels reared two chicks in their hole in the gable of the barn. Now that the young can fly fairly efficiently they have moved into the chestnut trees at the top of the field. No love is lost between the crows and the kestrels, and the two families avoid each other as much as possible.

The barn owls do not have the same problem, as they are not active until the other birds have gone to bed. They have reared one owlet, which seems to be perpetually hungry. The rasping, hissing sound begins about an hour before dark, and continues intermittently all night. If I go out at dusk I can see the owlet peering anxiously from the ventilation hole above our bedroom window, waiting for its parents to bring it a mouse. When it sees me the hissing stops and it retreats hurriedly out of sight, but soon it is back, hissing into the darkness.

There has been a dramatic change in the plants in bloom during the past two or three weeks. On the cliffs, and on the coastal slopes of Herm, a spectacular display of foxgloves has given way to bell heather, moon daisy and stonecrop. On the headlands and commons burnet roses are no longer flowering, but bird's-foot trefoil is in full bloom, its yellow flowers tinged with red, and on the dunes sea holly is just coming into flower.

Sea Holly, a coloniser of bare sand

Common gorse flowers practically all the year round but western gorse is beginning its flowering period now. It is a lower, more compact shrub than common gorse, with flowers of a deeper yellow. It is not common in Guernsey, but grows here and there on the clifftops, usually in the company of bell heather. In Jersey it is abundant on the cliffs near La Corbière, and at Grosnez, but the most I have ever seen is at Cap Fréhel in northern Brittany, where the deep gold of the gorse and the purple of the heather make a dazzling display over many acres of the headland.

Dodder, which often parasitises gorse, is also in flower now. It has no roots, leaves or green pigment of its own, but feeds by attaching itself to the branches of the host plant. The fine, red stems of the dodder form a dense mat which sprawls over the surface of the gorse bush, bearing rounded heads of pale pink flowers, smelling strongly of honey.

Dodder is not confined to gorse bushes, but sprawls over bell heather, Lady's bedstraw, bird's-foot trefoil and a number of other host plants. On Herm Common it grows on wild thyme and restharrow, its flowers adding to the delicious scents of the common.

In the garden the change has been no less dramatic. Violets, forget-me-nots, euphorbias of all sorts, gladioli, lilies and most of the roses have abruptly stopped flowering and their place has been taken by pansies, honeysuckle, agapanthus, phlox, dahlias, hydrangeas, myrtle and sweet peas. The change began at the end of June, and was dictated by day-length. As soon as the longest day was past the plants detected that the days were getting shorter, and acted accordingly.

Some flowers, like lawn daisies and geraniums, will cheerfully bloom at any time of the year. Most, however, are programmed to flower either when the days are getting longer or shorter. The 'long-day' plants have now finished flowering and have gone to seed, and it is the turn of the 'short-day' plants to bloom. Some of these, like buddleia, hemp agrimony and *Sedum spectabile*, are much sought after by butterflies and moths. At present our buddleia is attracting red admirals. Judging by their fresh condition, these have hatched locally, without having to make the long journey from the Mediterranean which their parents made in the spring.

The honeysuckle bush outside the kitchen door is in full bloom. The masses of light cream flowers are almost luminous in the dusk, and the sweet scent hangs on the air as darkness is falling. What kind of insect is it trying to attract?

I was always taught that honeysuckle is typical of plants pollinated by night-flying moths. The light colour shows up in the dark and the sweet scent, which is released as darkness falls, is attractive to moths. The sugary nectar, the bait which attracts the insects, is stored at the end of a long tube, and can only be reached by insects with a long tongue – again like moths. But have you ever actually seen a moth visiting a honeysuckle flower?

A Warwickshire botanist, writing in the newsletter of the Botanical Society of the British Isles, claims that in his part of the world the honeysuckle is pollinated by bumble-bees, flying during the day. Despite hours of watching, he has never seen a moth visiting the flowers. The young, white flowers first open in the evening, releasing a surge of scent. At first there is only a drop of nectar at the bottom of the tube, and an insect would need a proboscis 22mm long to reach it. The flower remains white for 48 hours, and during that time the nectar rises in the tube. On the third day the flower turns yellow. By then the nectar can be reached by an insect with a proboscis half the length. In Warwickshire there is one species of bumble-bee with a tongue long enough to reach the nectar on the first day, though others can reach it later.

Of course it does not follow that the same applies in Guernsey, and I once invited the readers of the local paper to tell me if they had seen any insects visiting honeysuckle flowers. They had. Honeysuckle is visited in broad daylight by humming-bird hawk moths. These intriguing insects behave exactly like the humming birds of the tropics, emitting a low hum as they hover about an inch away from the flower, and extending an extremely long proboscis to suck up the nectar.

Humming-bird hawk moths are migratory insects, which breed around the Mediterranean basin and spread northward each spring, reaching Guernsey in most years in June. If the summer is a good one they breed here as well, laying their eggs on various kinds of bedstraw. Sometimes they achieve two generations locally, before either migrating south, or attempting to hibernate. It is doubtful whether any survive the winter here.

Humming-bird hawk moths are unusual among moths in flying by day, and preferring bright sunshine. They are never particularly common in Guernsey but a few are seen every year, visiting a wide range of flowers. I have seen them in the garden feeding on giant echium flowers, and near the coast on sea radish.

One of the young bantam hens has just presented us with her second brood of the year. The six pale yellow balls of fluff follow her about, running when she clucks to indicate that she has found something edible. The mother bird can fly in and out of the hen run at will, and the chicks simply walk through the mesh of the wire, so they have the freedom of the garden. So far they have not done too much damage, although the hen's habit of scratching at leaves, to see if there are any interesting bugs underneath, does make rather a mess.

The bantams like to roost in the tree-tops, and every evening there is a commotion as the mother bird climbs a tree and tries to coax her chicks up after her. They are quite incapable of this, and in the end the hen comes down to earth, spreads her feathers and the chicks burrow into them for the night.

By the morning they are in the hen run with the other more conventional birds, waiting for breakfast. The hens have a strict social hierarchy, and woe betide anyone who tries to take food from a senior bird. Young chicks seem to have a special dispensation, and can even steal from the senior cock without being seen off.

The chicks born earlier in the year are no longer exempt. They are now gawky teenagers, at the bottom of the pecking order. They find this difficult to come to terms with, and when the mother bird clucks they still come running, only to find that they are no longer welcome. They will have to learn the hard way. When they are big enough they will test their strength, and one day one of them will be cock of the roost.

August

It is the peak of the tourist season, and the open spaces of the island are beginning to look a little jaded. Holidaymakers who come in April, May and June see the wild flowers at their dazzling best, and those who come in the autumn enjoy (if they are lucky) calm, golden days of great beauty. But by the beginning of August the coastal turf is very often dying of drought, and letters begin to appear in the local paper complaining of the 'weeds'.

The main flower along the west coast at this time of the year, and the cause of the most of the complaints, is sea radish. This is a rather leggy plant of the cabbage family growing to a height of about three feet. The flowers are yellow, or sometimes white, with four petals, and the fruit is a pod containing a row of bulging seeds.

Above: Dartford warbler on gorse with La Moye Point in background.

To be sure, sea radish has a slightly scruffy appearance, particularly when all the leaves have been eaten by snails, and only bare stalks and seed pods remain. But it is certainly not a weed. A weed is a plant growing in the wrong place. A sea radish in a potato patch would be a weed; on the cliffs and headlands it is a wild flower in its natural habitat. Its leaves are a source of food for snails and its flowers provide nectar for bees, moths and other insects. (Doubtless its fat seeds provide food for some animal, though I have to admit I don't know which).

The snail which strips the sea radish of their leaves, causing them to stand along the west coast like plucked chickens, is a comparative newcomer from the Mediterranean; the sandhill snail. It is sometimes called the Pisan snail, for the specimens that were used when the species was described scientifically came from Pisa. But it is widespread around the Mediterranean; and extends north as far as the south coast of England.

On a hot, sunny day you will have no difficulty in finding the sandhill snails, for they will be crowded at the tops of the radishes. While our native snails escape from the sun by burying themselves or hiding under stones, the sandhill snail, being used to Mediterranean conditions, gets as far away from the ground as it can.

The strongly-built shell is smaller and flatter than the common garden snail. It is sand-coloured, with a varying pattern of spiral or oblique, chevron-like markings.

Sandhill snails were introduced in 1860, when Dr. F.C. Lukis collected some in Jersey and released them at Vazon, Vale Castle and Bordeaux. The exotic snails did not like the east coast, but those at Vazon multiplied and spread along the coast in both directions, until today they can be found from Portinfer to L'Erée.

The sandhill snail serves as a good example of the danger of introducing an exotic animal without also introducing a predator to control it. Normally the snail does no harm, but occasionally the population reaches plague proportions, as it did in 1981 at Port Soif. In that long, hot summer, when they had consumed all the dune vegetation the snails moved inland and, operating mainly at night, ate everything in the gardens of Les Prins Estate.

If the climate really is changing and 'global warming' is not a temporary blip, exploited by the Greens for political reasons, we shall have to accept that the long summer droughts we have been experiencing in the last few years are here to stay. I'm beginning to think that this is the most powerful argument of all in favour of curbing the island's growing population, and calling a halt to development.

There is a strange belief among many Guernseymen that our water supply comes from the Pyrenees. I don't know who dreamt up the idea, or when, but it is an attractive notion, for it would mean we can use as much water as we like, without fear of running out. Unfortunately this is not the case. The water in our reservoirs, and in the ground, is the rain that has fallen on Guernsey. There is no other source. In recent years we have used more water than the rainfall has put back into the soil, with the result that the water table is falling. And the more we cover the island with roofs and tarmac, the more we reduce the area of soil that can absorb the rain.

Another consequence of the summer drought is the occasional heath fire. Cliffs and commons where there are old gorse bushes are extra vulnerable, for the old, dead branches and needles are tinder-dry, and it only takes a carelessly dropped cigarette, or the sun shining through a broken bottle to ignite them. Although these fires are frightening and dangerous, in the long term they serve to rejuvenate the gorse.

In the days when gorse was used as fuel in the bread oven which was built into the side of many a kitchen fireplace, it was treated as a crop and the cliffs and furze-brakes were cut in rotation. At any one time there would be some areas with mature bushes ready for cutting, some with half-grown bushes, and others where freshly-cut stumps were sprouting new growth.

This was beneficial to wildlife, for some creatures depend on soft, green gorse shoots. The rare Dartford warbler, which is slowly re-establishing itself in gorsey coastal areas after being nearly wiped out in the disastrous winters of 1988 and 1989, will not nest in old, leggy plants, but needs dense, green gorse bushes in which to breed. Now that nobody harvests the old bushes, nature solves the problem with the occasional furze fire.

In 1976 (the hottest, driest and sunniest summer on record), large areas of the cliffs from Petit Bôt to Le Prévôté were devastated by fire. Much of the National Trust property between La Corbière and Le Bigard was reduced to a bare, smouldering hillside, and for the first time it was possible to get a clear view of the walls which used to divide the sheep runs on the cliffs. The damage seemed catastrophic.

The following year there was a dazzling display of rosebay willow-herb, the plant which turned London's bomb-sites rose-pink during the Blitz. The plant is far from common in Guernsey, and had not been seen on the cliffs for some time, yet the seeds must have been waiting in the soil since the last fire. Then gorse seedlings began to germinate, and fresh, green shoots appeared from the charred stumps of the old bushes. Today gorse and broom again cover the ground, although isolated clumps of rosebay can still be found among the bushes.

The butterfly bush in the garden is in full bloom. It is close to the kitchen door, and on a sunny day swarms of butterflies and moths rise from the sprays of purple flowers every time you pass it. Buddleia is a survivor. If you cut it down to the ground it comes up better than ever, and its seeds carry it to unlikely places such as piles of builders' rubble, quarry faces and the tops of old walls, where it flourishes and scents the air.

Next to our buddleia is a clump of hemp agrimony, another

*Painted lady
on buddleia,
the 'butterfly bush'*

powerful magnet for butterflies. It grows to a height of four or five feet, and bears feathery heads of pink flowers which blend perfectly with the lilac-purple sprays of the buddleia. Hemp agrimony is a native wild plant, though not a very common one, and most gardeners would regard it as a weed. Ours sowed itself next to the buddleia, and is a very welcome addition to the garden. After flowering I shall cut it and the buddleia to the ground, and next year both will be back with renewed vigour.

Now that pesticides are more carefully controlled than they used to be, butterflies seem to be recovering from their catastrophic post-war decline. Those visiting the buddleia and hemp agrimony at present include red admiral, small tortoise-shell, large and small white and – most numerous of all – painted ladies. Other visitors include the silver-Y moth, the Jersey tiger, various hover-flies and at least three kinds of bumble bee.

When at rest, with wings closed, the painted lady is dark and almost invisible. When sunning itself with open wings it is brick red, with patches of black and white. In flight, the general impression is of a faded orange colour.

The painted lady is a migrant from North Africa and Arabia. Each spring it spreads northward through Europe and reaches Guernsey in April and May. It lays its eggs on thistles and nettles – a good reason for not being too severe with these weeds – and in a good year there may be two or three generations during the summer. The year 1996 was a particularly good one for painted ladies, and by August they were congregating in clouds around the buddleias. They do not hibernate; in the autumn some may attempt the return journey to Africa, but probably most will perish, and for next year's supply we will have to rely on fresh immigration.

Also attracted to the hemp agrimony and buddleia is the Jersey tiger. This large moth is a beautiful insect, flying by day as well as by night. In flight it resembles an orange butterfly, but when at rest the orange hind wings are covered by the tiger-striped forewings, held back in a delta shape. From a distance the markings appear as white stripes on a black background, although in fact the colours are pale cream and dark brown.

The caterpillars feed on low-growing wild flowers such as dandelion and deadnettle. They spend the winter as caterpillars, and continue feeding the following spring. Then they pupate and the new adults are the ones we are seeing now in the garden.

Despite its name the Jersey tiger is widespread in southern Europe, and reaches as far north as the south coast of England. Like the Jersey orchid, it is just as common in Guernsey as in the sister island.

In thundery weather in August the ants which share the house with us come out of their nest in the kitchen wall and swarm. Suddenly a whole generation has been born with wings, and the ability to use them. After milling about for a few hours on the gable of the house they take to the air, and we wonder who is going to have the pleasure of their company for the next year.

August thunderstorms can be heavy, with some surprising results. On the night of 22nd August, 1993, over an inch of rain fell in a few minutes. Dawn broke to reveal Shetland ponies in La Rue Sauvage standing up to their bellies in water, and in Les Baissières Mr. Brian Hodkinson found a 21-inch red mullet in his drive.

A long spell without wind is unusual in Guernsey, but it happens occasionally. A few weeks of calm, warm weather have at last raised the temperature of the sea to the point where one can enter it without becoming too blue. But to reach clear water one first has to negotiate a belt of flotsam, for the calm conditions have encouraged a lot of floating seaweed to accumulate in the bays.

Much of the weed is sea lettuce, a green seaweed which does indeed look like a floating lettuce leaf. The frond is thin and translucent, with wavy edges, and was originally attached to a rock by a short stalk. It is edible when boiled, but I would not advise putting it to the test, for it flourishes where fresh water, which may be none too clean, flows down the beach.

If the lettuce leaves are broken from their stalks by the waves they will continue to grow as they float in the sea, and in calm weather they tend to accumulate in the bays.

Mixed with the sea lettuce is another green weed, this time with tubular fronds a few inches long, and about the width of a pencil. It begins life attached to rocks in pools near the high-water mark, but like sea lettuce it breaks off and floats. Despite its abundance, it seems to have no English name – its Latin name is *Enteromorpha intestinalis*.

Knopper galls are beginning to fall from the oak trees and to lie on roads and garden paths. The irregularly shaped growths, resembling walnuts, are caused by a gall wasp which lays its egg in the acorn cup of the common English or pendunculate oak. As the wasp grub develops, it somehow manages to get the tree to produce a knopper gall instead of an acorn.

Knopper gall on oak

The gall is green, wrinkled and sticky at first, later becoming hard and black. Built into it can usually be seen the remains of the acorn that failed to develop. It spends the winter on the ground and in the spring the young wasp, always a female, climbs out and goes in search of a different kind of tree: the Turkey oak. She lays her eggs in its catkins, where they cause more galls, much smaller than the knoppers on the pendunculate oak. The wasps which emerge this time are of both sexes. After mating they fly to a pendunculate oak and the cycle is repeated.

Complicated life-cycles like this are quite common among parasites and gall-forming insects, but the need for two host trees limits this particular wasp to places where pendunculate and Turkey oaks grow together. In Guernsey the native tree is the pendunculate oak, but Turkey oaks, originally imported from eastern Europe, have been found to do well here. They don't seem to mind salt winds, and examples near the sea can be seen at the bus station and South Esplanade. In more sheltered places inland, such as Saumarez Park, there are some enormous specimens. The lobes of the leaf are pointed, not rounded as in the pendunculate oak, and the acorn cups are hairy.

Pendunculate oaks have been here for thousands of years and Turkey oaks for two hundred years or so, but the knopper wasp did not reach the island until the 1980s. At first it did so well and the galls were so prolific that there were hardly any viable acorns, and people began to worry about the future of the oak. Soon, however, the insect settled down and now in most years there are plenty of galls but also plenty of acorns.

Ivy broomrape flowers sporadically throughout the year, but August is the month when this slightly sinister plant is most in evidence. It appears almost overnight in hedges, at the foot of walls – anywhere, in fact, where there is ivy.

The stiff, purple stems, about a foot high, bear orchid-like flowers with an upper and a lower lip. The flowers are straw-coloured with a purple tinge, and the textbooks say they probably rely on self-pollination. But I have seen bumblebees visiting them, and I suspect that they are cross-pollinated in the usual way.

Broomrapes have no leaves or green pigment, for they are parasites, deriving their food from the roots of other plants. The rape in the name does not refer to the plants' anti-social habits, but to the turnip-like tuber at the base of the stem, by which the broomrape attaches itself to the roots of its host.

Of the ten British species of broomrape, by far the commonest in Guernsey is the one which attacks ivy. In the United Kingdom it is classified as a scarce plant, being almost confined to those parts of Wales and south-east England within the warming influence of the sea. Even in Jersey it is quite rare. But in Guernsey both ivy and its parasite are abundant.

Guernsey provides us with the first written record of ivy broomrape in the British Isles. It was found at Ivy Castle in 1726 by Thomas Knowlton, a professional gardener who had been sent to the island by the eminent physician and botanist James Douglas, to investigate the origin of the Guernsey lily. The diary of Knowlton's visit is preserved with Douglas's papers in Glasgow University library. On 8 June 1726 Knowlton wrote:

> .... walked out to see ye Ive Castle which lies about on mile and half [from town] being a large peace of grown inclosed by a wall and within it a moote sunk to raise a mount which is again enclosed by another wall with towers at proper distances which no doubt was formerly a strong place but now nothing but a pile of ruins and walls covered with ivy, which I suppose gives it the name and from the root of the ivy here grows Orobanca or Rape which is a very pretty plant and common in many places in England.

Ivy broomrape,
an attractive parasite

Château des Marais, a remote oasis among the marshes in Knowlton's day, is now surrounded by States houses and flats, the moat is silted up and more likely to contain derelict prams and supermarket trolleys than wild flowers. But in the ruins, the ivy and the broomrape are still there.

And the Guernsey lily … ? The legend had it that the beautiful flowers, of a deep rosy-pink, were first seen blowing among the dunes, after some bulbs had been washed up in a storm from a wrecked ship. The ship, and the bulbs, were supposed to have come from the far east.

We now know that *Nerine sarniensis* comes from South Africa. It has been associated with Guernsey since the 1650s, when a ship which had put in at the Cape ran aground off Guernsey. When she was re-floated the sailors gave some bulbs to a local landowner in return for his hospitality.

Knowlton found the lily flourishing in practically all the gardens he visited, and he reported that the more crowded the bulbs became, the better they seemed to flower. Today the Guernsey lily is treated as a greenhouse plant, and although hardier nerines are commonly grown in gardens, the true *N. sarniensis* is very rarely seen in the open. But if the tendency towards warmer summers and milder winters continues, it may once again become a feature of Guernsey gardens.

S eptember

The drought continues. In the hedges the elms (those that have not yet died of Dutch elm disease) are wilting, and in the fields the grass appears to be dead. Only the deep-rooted docks are looking happy. On the positive side, lawns have not needed mowing for over a month and autumn Lady's tresses are appearing in unexpected places.

Well over a hundred spikes of these small, white orchids have just appeared among the tombstones in St. Peter's churchyard. The dainty white flowers, smelling of almonds, are arranged spirally around a stem about six inches high. The Lady is the Virgin Mary; the tresses the flowers spiralling around the stem.

The leaves of the Lady's tresses are not borne on the stem, but in a rosette growing flat on the ground. Thus they are not damaged by the mowing machine. But in a wet summer the

Above: Woodpigeon on elder

flowering spikes would be mown with the grass before revealing themselves for what they are. Those in St Peter's churchyard must have grown there unseen for many years, but it is only after a long drought with no mowing that they have had a chance to flower.

In the wild, Lady's tresses grow in short grassland grazed by sheep or rabbits. There is a corner of Herm Common, grazed by rabbits, where I can usually find a few spikes at this time of year, but most of the Lady's tresses in Guernsey must be growing in lawns and churchyards.

On the cliffs there is very little colour. The heather is over. Even the gorse is having one of its rare periods with very few flowers, although the parasite dodder which sprawls over some of the gorse bushes has pink heads of honey-scented flowers.

The only plant to be flowering in any quantity is autumn squill. Singly, the short heads of tiny blue flowers with violet anthers would hardly be noticed. Collectively they impart a violet sheen to the short turf, otherwise now grey and dead, in which they grow.

The squills are not in the least upset by the drought which is killing the plants around them, for they are leafless at present. The curly, wiry leaves will appear after flowering. Like many other plants with a mainly Mediterranean distribution, the squill bulbs spend the summer in a dormant state, and the leaves are active in winter, when there is plenty of moisture.

The genetics of the autumn squill have been studied recently, for the bulbs contain a mucilaginous substance used in pharmacy. It turns out that the squills of Guernsey and Sark are of a distinct genetic race, known elsewhere only from west Cornwall. Those of Jersey and Alderney belong to a different race.

The related spring squill, though much commoner than autumn squill around the British coast, does not grow in the Channel Islands.

Lady's Tresses

Elderberries are ripening in the hedges, turning from red to glistening black, and already the birds are starting to feed on them. This morning I saw a fat wood pigeon trying to steal the berries from a bush in the garden. The bird was far too heavy for the twig it was trying to stand on, and eventually it gave up in disgust. The berries will be much enjoyed by the blackbirds, and next year elder seedlings will appear under all the bushes in which blackbirds like to sit while they digest their meals.

The birds seem to like elderberries more than any other fruit. Hips, haws and myrtle berries are left until February or March, by which time the birds are seriously short of food. But the elder bushes rarely retain their berries for more than a week after they have ripened.

Elder used to be credited with supernatural powers, and bushes are often to be found near old houses. One would be planted as close to the house as possible, for it was thought that it could not be struck by lightning. Ours is close to the kitchen door. Every winter I cut it to the ground, for it is far too close to the house to be allowed to grow into a tree. But it is a survivor, and each spring it comes up better than ever.

Another would have been planted near the dairy window, to deter witches from flying in and interfering with the butter-making. Butter would sometimes mysteriously refuse to turn, and you could not afford to take chances.

Judging by the number of droppings on the lawn, the garden is inhabited by at least one large hedgehog. The droppings are black. about two inches long and tapered at one end.

Gilbert White, the eighteenth century naturalist and vicar of Selborne, examined the droppings left by hedgehogs on his grass, and concluded that beetles formed a large part of their diet. He also described how they burrowed into his grass paths to eat the roots of the plantains. This met with his approval, for it destroyed a troublesome weed, although he wished they wouldn't leave craters all over his path.

I can find no evidence of beetles in the droppings on our lawn, and hope that the hedgehogs are devouring plenty of slugs instead. But something is helping itself to the windfall apples and pears, and this may account for the unusually large number and size of the droppings.

At this time of year hedgehogs have an instinct to eat all they can find, so that they can go into hibernation with a reserve of fat. In an average Guernsey winter, however, they never truly hibernate. They make a nest of fallen leaves in which they spend the day, and at dusk they emerge in all but the coldest weather, to snuffle around among the leaves and under bushes, looking for worms, woodlice and anything else they can find.

There are no early records of hedgehogs in Guernsey, and it is thought that they were introduced, probably by gardeners, in the early nineteenth century. They soon spread into the countryside and by the end of the century they were common everywhere. At first they were persecuted by farmers, probably because of the mistaken idea that they milked the cows in the fields. Today they are recognised as valuable controllers of pests, both in the fields and gardens.

Hedgehogs can move with surprising speed, and can easily climb walls and hedges. It is said that having reached the top of a wall they may not bother to climb down, but simply curl up and bounce. Despite their agility their reaction to danger is not to run, but to curl up and rely on their spines for protection. This is effective against animals but is no defence against a car, and dead hedgehogs are only too common on the roads.

At the top of the field which slopes up from our house is a row of sweet chestnuts. They are venerable trees, some with a girth of over ten feet. The chestnuts are just beginning to swell in their prickly cases, which practically cover the trees. In the evening light they are a beautiful sight, the light green chestnut cases standing out against the dark green foliage. Either because the water table has fallen over the years, or because of the exposed position, the topmost branches have died, and project grey and weathered above the trees, like stags' antlers.

The dead branches are much loved by the larger birds. For most of the year there is scarcely a moment when there is not a family of crows, magpies or kestrels sitting among the antlers, watching the field for carrion, beetles or voles as the case may be. At present, however, the antlers are full of starlings.

Throughout the breeding season the starlings were spread out over the countryside in pairs, building their untidy nests in holes in the trees, or under the eaves of houses and sheds. We had several pairs in the garden; you could tell where they were nesting by the pile of hay and grass they had dropped in the course of building the nest.

Now that they have finished breeding the starlings have become sociable, roaming the countryside in flocks. During the daytime there is often a small flock in the field digging for cockchafers, or sitting in the chestnut antlers. In the evening the flock becomes restless, taking off repeatedly, flying round, collecting more brids and returning. Finally it merges with a much larger flock of several thousand birds and disappears for the night. I don't know where the birds are roosting this year. A few years ago they chose the trees overhanging the bus station in town, where their droppings rendered the pavement so slippery that the authorities decided they must be evicted. All sorts of means, from hum-lines to music, were tried. Eventually, in their own time, the birds moved elsewhere.

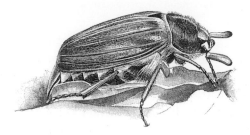

Cockchafer beetle

From a distance the starlings appear to be black, but when they come to the bird bath to have a splash it can be seen that they are beautifully spangled with purple, bronze and green. They have no particular song of their own, but are excellent mimics and are liable to repeat the song of any bird they have heard. Once I heard a curlew calling from the hen run. When I went to investigate the unlikely sound, it was coming from a starling which was sitting in a tree watching the chickens. This bird was probably on migration from further north, where it had been in contact with curlews, and it soon moved on. But another starling, which used to spend the summer regularly in our garden, learnt to imitate the telephone. When we were working outside we never knew if the ringing came from the bird or the real thing.

I have been giving the hedges their autumn trim. The Cutting of Hedges Ordinance, 1953, ordains that in the first half of June, and again in the second half of September, all hedges bordering public roads must be cut back and all overhanging branches removed to a height oftwelve feet. Furthermore, all clippings must be swept up and removed immediately.

All the cutting used to be done by hand with a sickle, leaving plenty of cuttings on the road to be cleared up. Now that labour is so expensive, it is cheaper to employ a contractor, who can do the job in a few minutes with a tractor-mounted flail machine. This also has the advantage of throwing most of the cut material back into the hedge. It is unusual nowadays to see anyone sweeping up in the lanes.

Some of our hedges lend themselves to being trimmed in this way, but where there is a vulnerable bank that may be damaged by the flail, I prefer to do the job by hand. Fortunately the well-balanced French hook, which was traditionally used in Guernsey, is still available in the island. It is an extremely effective tool, and I quite enjoy a morning or two swinging away at the undergrowth.

The autumn trim never involves as much work as the one in June. This year, after a dry summer, it was merely a matter of cutting a certain amount of hogweed and bracken, removing some brambles that were doing their best to cross the road, and sweeping up. For some reason the sight of me and my ancient Ferguson tractor causes a certain amount of merriment among the passers by.

❂

Rain at last. The continental high pressure system which has covered us for most of the summer has been seen off by an Atlantic low, and we are once again in a mild, damp, westerly airstream. It is not much more than a drizzle, but the ground is soaking it up gratefully and already, after just a few days, a haze of green is appearing on the lawn and in the fields.

Also appearing, as if by magic, are various mushrooms and toadstools. The familiar umbrella-shaped structures are merely the fruiting bodies of the fungus; the main part of the plant, consisting of a tangled mass of threads, is buried in the soil. Throughout the summer it has been feeding on leaf-mould, manure, or decaying roots in the soil, and forming buds at the surface. The autumn rain provides the water for these buds to expand, often overnight, into the fruiting bodies.

Until recently Guernsey has not been particularly noted for its fungi, but we are now beginning to realise that compared with most of continental Europe we have a rich variety. On the continent in recent years there has been a dramatic decline in mushrooms and toadstools, including many edible species that are collected commercially. Since poisonous species are disappearing as well, the decline is not simply the result of over-collecting. The cause seems to be pollution.

In Guernsey for most of the year the wind and rain come straight from the Atlantic. The purity of the air is demonstrated by the lichens. These strange composite plants, each one a partnership between a fungus and a green alga, are extremely sensitive to pollution. Here they grow luxuriantly on rocks, walls and trees – everywhere except close to roads where there are traffic fumes. It now appears that our fungi also are benefiting from the relative lack of pollution.

One of the largest and handsomest of the umbrella-shaped fungi is the parasol mushroom. The tall, straight stem may be a foot high and the cap, when fully open, curves gracefully out from a central prominence. The cap is covered in shaggy brown scales, and the gills beneath it are white. Both this and the closely related shaggy parasol are quite common in Guernsey. A clump of shaggy parasol mushrooms has just appeared under an elm tree in our garden. They are said to be edible, but we have decided we would rather look at them than eat them.

The same scruples do not apply to the field mushrooms which are popping up in the fields and even on the garden

Parasol mushroom

compost heap. These are very similar to the cultivated mushrooms of the supermarket, but are far tastier and are well worth collecting while they are young, before the maggots attack them. Unfortunately the deadliest toadstool of all, the death cap, is not unlike a field mushroom in appearance. So do invest in a good handbook before collecting fungi for the pot.

Field mushrooms like to grow in permanent pasture, where their underground threads can feed on cow and horse manure, brought down into the soil by dung beetles. In the same fields giant puffballs sometimes appear, looking unpleasantly like white skulls among the grass. In their young stage, when white and firm, they are edible, though not particularly exciting as a delicacy. They then go on to reach the size of a football before exploding, scattering a cloud of brown spores.

Giant puffballs used to be a rarity, but are increasing in numbers, both here and on the continent. They are not confined to pasture land; in May 1992 young Abigail Seabrook took one to school which she had found in her father's greenhouse at Les Sauvagées, St. Sampson's. It weighed in at five pounds, and measured 37 inches in circumference. In August of the same year a specimen at The Dell Nursery achieved a circumference of 49 inches. I don't know what the record is for Guernsey, but it is unlikely to equal a specimen from the USA (where else?) which appeared in the State of New York in 1877. It measured five feet four inches across, and was at first mistaken for a sheep.

Certain plants have charisma. A bee orchid on the coastal dunes, or a meadow of loose-flowered orchids, always excites interest and admiration. The Guernsey fern has charisma, not just because it is rare, but because it is elegant and quite unlike anything else. A fungus with charisma is the lattice fungus, *Clathrus ruber*. It is not common, but when it does appear in a hedge or under a tree, it always attracts attention.

The lattice fungus is a plant of southern Europe, whose range just reaches as far north as the Channel Islands and the milder parts of England. When young, the fruiting body resembles an egg. As it grows, the 'shell' bursts in such a way that it forms a hollow sphere of open latticework of a beautiful coral pink.

Lattice fungus, a rarity which always attracts attention

Unfortunately it attracts our attention not only by its appearance, but by its smell. The lattice fungus belongs to the stinkhorn family of fungi, whose spores are dispersed by flies attracted by a smell of rotting flesh. The pink, glutinous substance covering the lattice contains the spores, and exudes the aroma which flies find so attractive. Many a perplexed gardener, looking to see if something has died under his bushes, has been rewarded by the not very edifying sight of a stinkhorn, or the far more charismatic spectacle of a lattice fungus.

O c t o b e r

The rain of the last few weeks, coupled with the mild, muggy weather, has caused the grass to shoot up and already the lawn and the fields are lush and green. It is difficult to believe that three weeks ago we were suffering from a prolonged drought.

Now is the time when gardening columnists in the national newspapers tell us we should be oiling our mowing machines and putting them away for the winter. There is no chance of that here; our machine has not been so busy since the spring.

In the field, a bunch of heifers are enjoying the grass. The autumn flush looks lush and green and appetising, but lacks the nutritional value of spring grass. Also, being composed mainly of water, it is laxative, and our grandchildren are even more likely than usual to get covered in manure.

Both heifers and grandchildren are enjoying the chestnuts,

Above: Curlew, a shy winter visitor

which are beginning to fall at the top of the field. First they have to be extracted from their extremely prickly cases. The children use the heels of their boots, but the cows have to rely on their sensitive lips to part the cases. They screw up their eyes in pain, but the sweet chestnuts are worth the agony.

Dews are heavy at this time of year, and sometimes in the morning the field appears to be covered by fine threads of gossamer, made visible as the drops of water that have condensed on them reflect the sun. Money spiders are so small that they are not usually noticed, although there may be a million in an acre of grassland. In the autumn the minute creatures climb to the top of a blade of grass or a twig, and each pays out a fine thread of gossamer. If there is an upcurrent of air, as there often is on a sunny morning, the gossamer carries the the spider into the air, and the species is thus dispersed.

The dew also shows up the intricate web spun by the diadem spider. In the morning the spider will be hanging, head down, in the centre of the web it has spun the night before. It is a beautiful creature, with a pattern of white spots in the shape of a cross on its abdomen. The body of the female is about half-an-inch long; the male is much smaller. In our garden the diadem spiders like to sling their webs across a path, or even across a doorway, where they are almost bound to be destroyed during the course of the day. But by the next morning a shining new web will be in place.

An exotic cousin of the diadem spider that has only been in the island for two or three years is sometimes called the wasp spider, for its abdomen and legs are vividly striped in black and yellow. It is a native of southern Europe, which has been extending its range northwards in recent years. Presumably young wasp spiders parachuted to the island from France on threads of silk, and now several are reported each year. The wasp-like colours would make birds think twice before eating them. They certainly look rather alarming, although in fact they are harmless.

The web, which is slung between tussocks of grass, is similar to the diadem spider's except that there is a conspicuous zig-zag band above and below the hub. Near the web the female spins a flask-shaped egg case of silk, about an inch in diameter.

Diadem Spider

I don't know which kind of spider frightened Miss Muffet. It was not a wasp spider, for they did not reach the British Isles until four hundred years after the incident commemorated in the nursery rhyme. It might have been a diadem spider, or more likely one of the large black house spiders that we tend to meet in the bath. She was not alone in being terrified of these harmless and useful creatures.

Dr. Thomas Muffet was a sixteenth century naturalist who thought spiders were a cure for practically all ills. He used cobwebs to staunch the flow of blood from a wound (this really does work, but please don't think I am recommending it), and to reduce fever he prescribed spider sandwiches. Perhaps his daughter Patience's fear of spiders was the result of being made to eat them.

The ivy started to flower at the end of September, and is now in full bloom and attracting numerous insects of various kinds.

Ivy is unusual in having two quite distinct ways of growing. Young shoots cling closely to the tree or wall they are using as a support, and bear the familiar three-pointed ivy-shaped leaves. Shoots that grow from a mature plant do not cling, but grow away from the support, and branch to form dense bushes, almost like trees themselves. The leaves of these mature shoots are rounded, without points except at the tip. It is these dense, mature bushes that are now covered in round heads of yellow-green flowers.

Ivy flowers; a late feed for bees

The flowers have small insignificant petals, but the protruding yellow stamens are quite conspicuous. Insects visit the flowers for the nectar, which glistens on the surface of the flowers and is easily licked up by insects with short tongues.

Ivy flowers provide an important late meal for hive bees, which by this time of the year are beginning to run out of flowers to visit. The flavour of ivy honey is not particularly good, and most bee-keepers are happy to leave it for the bees' own use during the winter.

In the last year or two there have been very few hive bees about, for they are still recovering from the ravages of a parasitic mite, Varroa. The disease is sweeping through Britain and reached

Guernsey in 1992, wiping out many of the hives. Fortunately it can be controlled by chemical means.

A bee of similar size, but with a more strongly striped abdomen than the hive bee, is visiting the ivy in force at present. This is a burrowing bee, which forms colonies in dry, sandy banks, often beneath a hedge where there is a convenient supply of ivy nectar. Each female digs an individual burrow, and has to make many journeys to provision it with honey for her young.

This bee is very similar to another that appears earlier in the year and feeds on sea aster, and until recently it was thought that the two belonged to the same species. We now know that they are distinct. The late ivy-feeding bee has been given the name *Colletes hederae* (the ivy-burrowing bee). It is common in the Channel Islands but has not yet been found in the United Kingdom.

❂

Driving along the coast road the other day I came face to face with a magnificent flowering specimen of *Agave americana,* the Mexican aloe or century plant. Soaring from behind the wall at Fort Saumarez was what appeared to be a giant stick of asparagus about twenty feet in height. From the upper part of the stem horizontal branches spread out, turning up at the ends to bear bunches of yellow flowers.

The plant had obviously been flowering for some time and some of the bunches were already over, but those still in bloom had enormous yellow anthers projecting from the flowers, which were attracting a number of red admiral butterflies.

The agave is native in Central America, but has been grown in gardens in the Channel Islands and the Isles of Scilly for many years. The Victorians were fond of it, and in 1878 Victor Hugo had a 25 feet specimen in his garden at Hauteville. As gardens became smaller it went out of favour but it persists in some old gardens, and always attracts attention when it flowers. In the 1920s Compton Mackenzie caused it to be planted in Herm, where it still grows in the quarry above Fisherman's Cottage.

The agave is sometimes called the century plant because of the mistaken belief that it flowers only once in a hundred years. Each plant certainly only flowers once in its life, but this may be as early as ten years after planting, though it is often much longer.

Until the flowering year the plant consists of a rosette of cactus-like leaves, with sharp teeth at the edges and tip. The rosette grows larger each year until the leaves are about three feet long. Finally it sends up a flowering stem which extends to 20 or 30 feet in a few weeks. After flowering the plant dies, but not before it has sent out offshoots which grow into new rosettes.

With a succession of mild winters and dry summers in recent years the agaves seem to have been flowering more frequently than they used to. In 1991 one flowered at the Ivy Gates for the first time for more than fifty years. In the same year two rosettes flowered in the quarry in Herm, and others have flowered in most subsequent years.

Agave Americana at Fort Saumarez

In a corner of our garden is a dense bed of nettles. Our excuse for leaving the nettles unmolested is that they will provide food for the caterpillars of various butterflies and moths. I cannot honestly say that I have ever seen any caterpillars on them, but they are made use of from time to time by the bantams.

The chickens have a perfectly good hen house, and the larger birds are happy to retire to it for the night. But the bantams are independent birds, and insist on roosting in the trees. Even when there is a westerly gale blowing up from the coast, they climb high into the trees which overhang the hen run, and spend the night among the swaying branches. In the morning they come flapping down to earth, and if they land the wrong side of the wire, they follow my wife into the run when she gives them their breakfast.

Three weeks ago Susanna, the senior bird, went missing. She was not in the run, and failed to turn up for her meals. Like her namesake in 'The Marriage of Figaro', she is a bossy bird, and the other hens were only too glad to be left in peace, but my wife decided that she must be found. Eventually we saw her beady eye glaring at us from the nettle bed. She was sitting on nine eggs. These have now hatched, and nine chicks are peeping out from under her feathers.

October is not the ideal time of year to be born into the world. The advantage of a late hatching is that the young hens should start laying next year when their older sisters are having a break. The problem is that for some reason these 'blackberry chicks' are more likely to be cocks than hens. One October we had a family of sixteen chicks, and every one of them was a cock.

In the hedges and fields, and beside the cliff paths, the lobed leaves of alexanders are appearing among the grass. Each leaf has three lobes, which are again divided into three. This is the cow parsley-like plant which flowers so abundantly in the early spring. Like many Mediterranean plants, alexanders like to grow through the winter, when there is plenty of moisture, and lie dormant in the summer drought.

Alexanders are biennial; some of the leaves we are seeing now belong to young seedlings that have just germinated, while others are second-year plants growing from tap-roots which have been resting during the summer. They will grow throughout the winter and flower in February or March, when the lanes will be lined by the glossy green plants, with umbels of yellow-green flowers.

Also appearing now are the arrow-head leaves of another Mediterranean plant, large lords-and-ladies. The leaves and strange arum-like flowers of the large species are similar to those of the common native lords-and-ladies, and for most of the year the two are difficult to tell apart. The leaves of the large species never have black spots, but for some reason the common lords-and-ladies of Guernsey usually lack the black blotches which decorate the leaves of the same plant in England. Fortunately the leaves of common lords-and-ladies do not appear until January, so now is the time to find the large species: any wild arum with leaves visible between now and Christmas will be large lords-and-ladies.

Although its headquarters are in the Mediterranean region, it is possible that large lords-and-ladies is native in Guernsey. It is more likely that it was introduced in Elizabethan times, when it was grown for the starch contained in the tubers. This was used in laundering the elaborate linen of the period. In England it was cultivated for this purpose, particularly on the Isle of Portland, and it still persists here and there near the south coast. Certainly in Guernsey, although it is not rare in the wild, it is mainly to be found near old houses.

The autumn migration is in full swing. On a still night you can hear the fluting call of waders overhead, as they keep in touch while flying southward through the darkness. The hedges, woods and reed beds are full of birds, resting and feeding before continuing their journey. Their presence is not immediately obvious, for they are keeping a low profile. In the garden the resident thrushes, blackbirds and tits have been joined by others passing through. Many more great and blue tits are visiting the bird table than the two or three pairs we normally see, and the other morning I woke to find a party of long-tailed tits busily hunting for insects in the lilac tree outside the bedroom window.

There are more birds in the island now than at any other time of year. In the spring the influx of birds travelling north is less spectacular as it is spread over a longer period, and consists only of birds that have survived the winter. By contrast the autumn migration consists not only of adult birds, but all their young as well, all hurrying to escape the northern winter.

Guernsey is well placed to watch this mass movement, being on one of the main migration routes up and down the western fringe of Europe. With the wide tide range, and large areas of sand and rocks exposed at low tide, the island is particularly popular with migrating waders. About twenty-five species of wading birds, which earn their living between the tidelines, visit us on migration. For some of them this is the end of the journey, and they stay with us for the winter. From now until spring, a visitor to almost any of the bays and headlands around the east, north or west coast will be rewarded by the sight of parties of turnstone, dunlin, ringed plover, oystercatcher and many others, busily foraging among the rocks or probing the sand at the edge of the sea.

In the summer the beaches are too full of the human species to expect to see many waders. Yet even on such popular tourist beaches as L'Ancresse and Vazon there are usually parties of turnstone, dunlin or ringed plover running around at the water's edge, or flying in tight formation to another part of the beach when disturbed.

These summer parties are of young, non-breeding birds. They live a carefree existence, flying out to rest on the outlying rocks when the tide is high, and spreading out on the exposed sand, rocks and pools to feed when it is low. However, since 1980 a few pairs of ringed plover have nested on the west coast. Sometimes they have been successful in rearing young, but all too often the shingly beaches on which they breed have been disturbed by walkers, or even four-wheel drive vehicles, and the eggs, which look exactly like pebbles, have been destroyed.

Apart from these few diminutive ringed plovers, the only waders to breed regularly round our shores are the much larger oystercatchers. These are the black and white birds with long, orange bill and pink legs, which fly fussily around, piping loudly, when they think somebody is getting too close to their nest. They breed low on cliffs, and on isolated rocks all round the coast. Most of the off-islets have a pair, often nesting in the turf, near its edge where the rocks begin.

But that was in the summer. Now the resident oystercatchers have been joined by numerous others which have been breeding further north, and have stopped to refuel on our beaches. Many will decide to stay; in the winter it is not uncommon to see parties of a hundred or more on the offshore reefs.

Oystercatchers no doubt eat oysters when they get the opportunity, but their main diet is cockles and limpets. They can detach a limpet from a rock with a sharp sideways blow from the powerful orange bill.

In the winter the oystercatchers often form mixed parties with curlews. These are the largest waders of all, with streaky brown plumage and an extremely long, down-curved bill. They are shy, and keep well away from people, but their evocative, liquid call carries over long distances. They can often be seen wading in shallow water at the bottom of the beach, probing for worms with their immensely long bills. As the rising tide begins to cover the causeway to Hermetier, the islet to the north of Herm harbour, a party of curlews often assembles, to follow the water as it laps over the mud.

It is much easier to get close to a turnstone. This splendid little wader, slightly bigger than a ringed plover, has little fear of man. It is often to be seen in the harbours and on the slipways, energetically flicking pieces of seaweed aside as it searches for sandhoppers. On the shore it earns its name by turning over pebbles, bending its knees to push its short, stout bill under the stone and jerking it over, then darting to catch any creature that has been exposed.

In the winter the turnstone has a mottled grey back, a white belly with a broad dark band on the breast, and orange legs. The Guernsey shoreline is considered to be of international importance for wintering turnstone. This means that a significant proportion of the world population of these little waders spend the winter with us.

November

We have had several weeks of stormy weather and heavy showers. A series of depressions has raced across the Atlantic and, instead of passing to the north of us, as they often do, they have aimed straight for us. As a result there has been very little autumn colour, for the leaves have been blown from the trees before having a chance to colour. The sycamores lost theirs some weeks ago, then ash, followed by oak and sweet chestnut. Now even the limes, which usually colour well, are bare. Only the Guernsey elms are still clinging stubbornly to their leaves.

In the garden the soil is too wet for digging, but we have been kept busy raking up and composting the leaves. In the fields I have been taking the opportunity to cut back the growth of some of the internal hedges. The roadside hedges have to be trimmed by law, but the law says nothing about internal hedges, which

Above: Magpies, nature's scavengers

therefore tend to be neglected. They slowly extend out into the field until they are taking up so much room that something has to be done. So I have been slashing back the brambles and elm suckers until I have reached the hedgebank, but leaving as thick a hedge as possible on top of the bank.

Guernsey's network of hedgebanks dividing the small fields, and bordering narrow lanes, is one of the features that give the island such a strong character of its own. The Pennines and the Cotswolds have dry-stone walls, the Midlands have hedges planted at ground level, with a ditch on either side, and parts of Wales have upended slabs of slate. Only in Devon and Cornwall, Brittany and Normandy will hedgebanks similar to those in the Channel Islands be found. Even between Jersey and Guernsey the hedges differ, both in the construction of the banks and the plants growing on them. Sark, which was colonized from Jersey in the sixteenth century, has hedges of the Jersey type; in Alderney the fields have never been enclosed by hedges.

Many of the hedgebanks are at least four hundred years old and some, particularly those along the parish boundaries, may have seen the last millennium. In England, most of the open fields and the common land were enclosed in the eighteenth century. In Guernsey the enclosures came earlier than this, probably mainly in the reign of Elizabeth I. William Camden, writing in 1586, claimed that there were very few open fields left in Guernsey. By the time the first accurate survey of the island was published, in 1787, the whole island had been enclosed, with the exception of L'Ancresse Common and the cliffs and headlands.

It is now possible to check the history books by botanical means, thanks to a happy discovery by Dr. Max Hooper of Monks Wood experimental station. After sampling numerous hedges in various parts of England, he discovered that the more kinds of trees and shrubs a hedge contains, the older it is likely to be. Moreover, in a thirty-yard length of hedge there will be on average one species of tree or shrub for every hundred years of the hedge's life.

This may seem too good to be true, but it has been tested many times, and has proved remarkably reliable – at least in England. With our rather different history of land use it does not follow that it would work in Guernsey, although a few counts of trees in our own hedges suggest that it does.

One of our fields is triangular, the original field having been cut diagonally in half by one of General Doyle's military roads in 1810. The roadside hedge, which was presumably constructed soon afterwards, contains on average two tree species in each thirty-yard length. By contrast a cart track, which was already there when the survey of 1787 was made, is bounded by hedges which have an average four and four-and-a-half species per thirty-yard length. This would indicate that the fields each side were enclosed before the end of Elizabeth's reign.

Two or three years ago at this time of year, an anguished letter appeared in the local paper, complaining that not a single gorse flower was to be seen on the bushes on L'Ancresse Common. There is a saying that when the gorse is not in flower, kissing is out of fashion. The implication is that there is never a time of year when there is no blossom on the gorse. In Guernsey folklore there is a story of a man who, on his deathbed, got his wife to promise that she would not marry again while there was blossom on the furze. After twelve months the widow had discovered that there is not a day in the year when the gorse was not in bloom.

Common gorse has its peak of flowering in the spring, when the bushes are literally covered with golden blooms. As the blossom fades the pods develop, and during the summer they explode on hot days, when the two halves of the pod twist apart and flick out the seeds. Already, while this is going on, new flower buds are developing, ready to open whenever the weather allows. In our mild climate they usually begin to open in the late summer, and the gorse continues to flower throughout the winter.

*Gorse, in flower
all year round*

The year the letter appeared, the flowers on the common were held back for some reason. However, some bushes on the south cliffs were flowering, and I was able to reassure the writer that kissing was still in fashion.

The old saying is particularly true in western Britain and the Channel Islands, because there is another species, western gorse, which has its main flowering time in late summer and autumn, when common gorse is seeding. Western gorse forms smaller, more compact bushes than common gorse, and the flowers are a deeper gold. It grows on acid cliff-top heaths, where it makes a glorious show with the purple of the bell heather. Unfortunately it is not common in Guernsey, although it grows here and there round the coast, and in Herm.

More gales, and more heavy showers are coming at us from the Atlantic. Although we are more than half a mile from the sea the windows are encrusted with salt, and at last the elms are losing their leaves.

It is tragic that so many of the elms are now dead or dying. The lethal strain of Dutch elm disease, which has killed most of the elms in southern England, reached Guernsey in 1977. Eight out of every ten trees in the hedgerows were elms. They were such an important element in the landscape, and so valuable in sheltering houses, glasshouses and crops, that the States decided to try to contain the disease, to give time for replacement trees of other species to become established. By felling and burning every infected tree, the loss of elms over the following ten years was limited to one per cent per year.

Then there was a series of long summer droughts, which weakened the elms and allowed the disease to spread faster than the felling programme, or the budget, would allow. The programme was abandoned in 1992, and now well over half the elms are either dead or infected.

Now that the leaves have fallen from the survivors, it can be seen that the elms are of two distinct types. One is a stiffly upright tree, with a straight trunk and branches ascending at a steep angle. At the tips the twigs turn to point vertically upwards. The leaves are small and not easily damaged by the wind. Because of its compact method of growth, it is a good tree for cities and municipal parks, and is included in many nurserymen's catalogues. I have seen it flourishing as far north as Glasgow, where with luck the climate will prove too cold for the elm bark beetle which carries the disease. I am sorry to say it is usually sold by UK nurserymen as the Jersey elm. This is definitely a misnomer, for the few specimens that did exist in Jersey before the disease struck were supplied by the Caledonia Nursery, Guernsey. It is the Guernsey elm.

The other type is a more floppy tree, with a leaning trunk and spreading branches which tend to droop at the ends. It has larger leaves than the Guernsey elm, and is thought to be a hybrid between it and the wych elm This hybrid elm is also common in Normandy, and was probably brought from there along with the Norman varieties of cider apples, when cider production became an important industry in the seventeenth century. They were planted in the hedgerows to shelter the apple trees.

It used to be thought that the upright Guernsey elm was introduced at the same time. But it is not found in Normandy, and apart from planted specimens in English parks, the only place where it grows in any quantity is Guernsey. So it is now accepted that the Guernsey elm is indeed the native elm of Guernsey.

Both varieties are equally susceptible to Dutch elm disease, and it would be a tragedy if they were allowed to become extinct in the island. I don't think this will happen, for elms are great suckerers, and the hedges are full of shoots which have arisen from the stumps and roots of felled trees. Sometimes the suckers spring up and immediately die of the disease, but often they survive. Experience in Cornwall, where the elms are closely related to ours, suggests that they will reach a height of about twenty feet before being attacked by the elm bark beetle and contracting the disease.

Mature elms will soon be a thing of the past in Guernsey, but with luck there will always be smaller ones, providing shelter and shade in the hedges.

❂

Introducing an alien animal into the wild is always a risky business. It may fail to find enough food, or fail to achieve a viable breeding population, and die out. More dangerously, it may find food in abundance and breed so successfully that it becomes a pest, particularly if there is no natural predator to keep it under control.

The Norman seigneurs who introduced rabbits as a source of fresh meat, and kept them closely guarded in their *garennes*, had no idea that they would escape and become a major pest, grazing crops intended for cattle, barking trees, and reaching every corner of the island, including all the off-islets.

Sometimes an animal is introduced by accident, or reaches the island by some unknown means. In 1985 some small, shrimp-like animals were noticed among fallen leaves in a garden in Collings Road. They were about half an inch long and moved by hopping, in exactly the same way as the familiar sand-hoppers we see on the beach, leaping as they follow the rising tide up the sand.

Sand-hoppers do not penetrate more than a yard or two inland, and no land-living relatives were known in Europe. The animals eventually turned out to be landhoppers (sometimes called woodhoppers) from either Australia or New Zealand – nobody seems quite sure which. They are thought to have been brought to Britain accidentally in the containers of nursery plants, and are now quite common in Devon, Cornwall and some other parts of the country, including Kew Gardens. Presumably they came to Guernsey with nursery stock from the UK.

Before long landhoppers were being seen in other gardens, and then they began to invade the outlying parts of the island. They reached our garden in 1994, when I found three hiding under my boots outside the back door. They immediately dived for cover under the doormat. Now I can always find several by turning over a stone, or moving a pile of leaves.

Landhoppers are very like their relatives the woodlice, except that they are compressed from side to side, rather than from top to bottom. Like woodlice their shells are not waterproof, and they avoid the drying action of the sun by hiding under stones and leaves. At night they come out to feed, and have a habit of squeezing under doors into houses, and dying in shoals on the carpet or under the radiator. Apart from this slight nuisance they don't seem to do any harm.

Nobody knows what the landhoppers are eating, but whatever it is there must be plenty of it, for they are now abundant all over the island. They in turn would provide plenty of food for a predator. I have not yet seen a bird eating them – perhaps our garden hedgehog has discovered them, and that is the reason for the unusually large droppings on the lawn.

A few years ago I could count on seeing at least one bat flitting about in the dusk if I went out just as darkness was falling. They would fly to and fro in the space between the house and the trees, turning sharply at the end of each run and repeating the circuit over and over again in their search for night-flying insects. They would be out every night in the summer, and on mild nights in the winter as well. Some were pipistrelles, and others the slightly larger long-eared bats.

I still see bats occasionally, but can no longer rely on seeing them. Numbers have declined everywhere in the last few years, and Guernsey is no exception. The main problem is the loss of the secluded places where they spend the daylight hours, and where they hibernate in severe weather. Barns are converted into houses and hollow, ivy-covered trees are cleared away. Quarries are filled in, and their ivy-covered sides are no longer bat refuges. On the positive side, the chemicals used in the treatment of roof timbers are no longer lethal to bats, so as long as they have access to the roof-space, they should be able to make use of houses once more.

Pipistrelle bat

I was particularly delighted, therefore, to see a pile of moth wings, and a sprinkling of black pellets like large mouse droppings, on the floor of the barn a few days ago. I could see no sign of a bat among the rafters above, but one had obviously been there, and by the size of the droppings it was larger than a pipistrelle. When I went to lock up after dark, I shone the torch into the roof, and there, hanging from a rafter, was a long-eared bat. He twitched his enormous ears at me and I hurriedly switched off the torch and left him to eat his moth in peace.

The bat is never there in the daytime, and must retire to some other roosting-place, probably in company with other bats. But at night I often find him in the barn. Presumably he hangs from the rafters to consume his latest catch, before continuing his search for food.

The large ears are a sonar listening device. Bats are not as blind as people suppose, but to catch insects and avoid obstacles in the dark they use echo-sounding. Men like to think that they invented this, but it was perfected by bats many millions of years before we existed.

It has recently been recognised that the long-eared bat is in fact two species: a brown kind, widespread in Britain, and a grey continental species. Nearly all the long-eared bats found in Guernsey so far have belonged to the continental race. But the differences are small, and the only way to be sure is to find a dead one. Occasionally dead greater horseshoe bats are also found, with a sonar device resembling a horse-shoe on the tip of the nose. These were probably not born in the island, but strayed here from France.

The heifers have nearly finished grazing the field next to the house, and apart from a few patches of nettles, which they avoid, it is like a lawn. They will happily eat nettles when they have wilted, so the answer is to go out on a sunny morning with a hook, and cut them while the heifers are still in the field. At the top of the field the first daffodil leaves have appeared among the grass, and are six inches high already. These earliest leaves belong to a variety called 'Paperwhite', a scented narcissus with small pure white flowers, several to a stem. In the garden the leaves of two other multi-headed narcissi are well up; 'Grand Primo', white with a lemon centre, and the bright orange 'Soleil d'Or'. All three varieties are descended from Mediterranean species, and begin growing as soon as the soil becomes moist in the autumn. With luck there will be some flowers for Christmas.

A plant that is coming into flower now is the Guernsey lily, *Nerine sarniensis*. Its hardy relation, *N. bowdenii*, has been flowering since the middle of October, and the clumps of sugar-pink flowers are still the brightest feature of the garden. But now the pure red flowers of the true Guernsey lily are opening. The flowers, grouped in a head on a long, slender stem, have narrow, slightly crimped petals, and protruding stamens.

The sweet violet, a much humbler flower, but equally beautiful, is also beginning to bloom. The flowers are a deeper violet colour than the common dog violet, and they are sweetly scented. The leaves, which are rounded at the tips, form dense masses on the ground, and would cheerfully take over all the flower beds if allowed to do so. In the orchard sweet violets grow under the apple trees, and don't object to the mowing machine in the least.

Sweet violet is a native wild flower, blooming in woods and on hedgebanks, but it has also been cultivated for many centuries. I remember bunches being picked and sent to Covent Garden. It will continue to bloom throughout the winter, until the dog violet, with paler flowers and pointed leaves, takes over in the spring.

At the beginning of the month the ivy flowers were attracting, among other insects, numerous wasps. Now the ivy has nearly finished flowering, and most of the wasps have died. Unlike bees, wasps do not have overwintering colonies. All the workers and males die at the end of the season, and only the queens remain alive through the winter. The queens, much larger than the workers we are used to seeing during the summer, are now looking for a quiet, dry corner in which to hibernate. If every queen survives the winter and starts a colony, we are going to have an awful lot of wasps next year.

We have no objection to wasps, for they are extremely efficient hunters and keep other insects, including flies, under control. The trouble is that most of the queens come into the house, and their ambition is to hide between the folds of the curtains. This would be acceptable if only they would stay there, but when we light a fire or switch on the heating they wake up and start bumbling around the room. So we collect them up and consign them to one of the outbuildings, where they will not be disturbed by the heat.

D e c e m b e r

The weather continues mild, with clear, fine days alternating with dull days of drizzle and mist. I have been taking advantage of the fine days to mow the rough grass in front of the house, before the daffodil leaves appear. When once they are up I shall not be able to mow the grass again until the daffodil leaves die down in the early summer.

In the field it is a different matter. The heifers think daffodil leaves taste disgusting and leave them severely alone, carefully grazing the grass between them. Later, when the daffs begin to flower, we will banish the heifers from the field. We once had a cow called Stella (she had a white star on her forehead) whose idea of bliss was to wander round the field, carefully nibbling off the flowers. Apparently they tasted better than the leaves. Not only did we lose the flowers, but we nearly lost Stella, who

Above: Robin, a much-loved resident

went down with bloat. This is an extremely distressing condition in which the stomach blows up with gas, which is unable to escape in the usual way because bubbles of foam in the gullet prevent belching. In the old days the farmer would simply release the gas with a pitchfork, but a less drastic remedy is to dose the animal with a mixture of turpentine and linseed oil. A pint of this evil-tasting mixture has to be poured down the throat of the unwilling animal. When Stella sneezed, the result can be imagined.

Daffodil leaves contain a lot of sticky juice, and in June, when we mow the field for hay, it is extremely difficult to get them dry enough to bale. Once dry, however, they become a delicacy. The cows prefer hay containing daffodil leaves to any other. Unfortunately it can still cause bloat.

The mild weather has caused a number of plants to spring into growth. This is particularly true of those introduced from warmer climes, which are programmed to be most active in winter, when there is plenty of moisture in the soil. The leaves of alexanders and three-cornered garlic, from the Mediterranean, are already well up in the hedges. In the garden arum lilies from South Africa, giant echiums from Tenerife, giant geraniums from Madeira and pittosporum bushes from New Zealand are all growing actively. All are tender, and their presence in Guernsey is something of a lottery. They would be cut back or even killed by a severe frost; fortunately this is a rare enough event for the risk of growing them to be worth taking.

With the soil as wet as it is I am keeping off the vegetable garden as much as possible, but I have managed to plant the shallots, which like to start growing before Christmas. I have also sown a row of broad beans. These should germinate at once, and will be six inches high by the New Year.

With the ground too wet for digging, and most of the leaves swept up and consigned to the compost heap, what better way to spend a short but sunny day than exploring the island's green lanes?

The 'Richmond map' of 1787 shows a labyrinth of narrow lanes, substantially unchanged since the middle ages. Twisting between the fields and following the valleys, the lanes still form the basis of the island's road system. Early in the present century most were surfaced with tarmac and became accessible to motor traffic. A surprising number, however, have never been given a hard surface. There are about fifty of these green lanes, some wide enough for a horse and cart and some with barely enough width for a pedestrian. They escaped the tarmac either because they were too narrow, or too little used, to justify the expense of surfacing. Today they are recognised as a positive asset to the island, for they are ideal for walking without risk from traffic, and there is an outcry whenever the authorities attempt to surface one.

Most of the green lanes are only a few hundred yards long, and to make a round journey you have to include a few stretches of hard road. Nevertheless, with a map and a little ingenuity it is possible to devise innumerable walks through countryside which is never seen by those who stick to the main roads.

Some green lanes were left as backwaters when the main roads were improved at the time of the Napoleonic wars. Until 1810 a journey between St. Peter Port and the outlying parts of the island was a major undertaking. Most Guernseymen were quite content with this state of affairs, but the Lieutenant-Governor of the time, Gen. Sir John Doyle, was concerned that if the French landed he would be unable to get his troops to the scene in time. With considerable tact he managed to persuade the States and the landowners to allow him to straighten and widen some of the roads, and give them a hard surface.

The French never landed, but Doyle's military roads proved of immense value; they are still the main arteries of the island. A footpath was provided on one side for the full length of each road, and distances from the Town Church were marked by milestones of grey granite. Most of the milestones are still there – the highest numbered is the seven-mile stone, opposite Les Adams Chapel. Where a road was straightened a disused dog's-leg was left, and many of these remain as secluded green lanes.

Several of the green lanes radiate from the medieval parish churches. At St. Saviour's a grassy path crosses the churchyard to the west of the church, and descends the escarpment between high, shady banks. After crossing two roads it continues towards the reservoir. Before the dam was completed in 1947 it continued down to the coast at Perelle.

Another green lane leaves from the south of the church. Two or three steps lead down from the churchyard, and beside them is a set of rough stone seats. This is the feudal court of Fief Jean Gaillard, where in the middle ages the officials of the lord of the manor would collect feudal dues in the form of corn or chickens. From here the footpath, paved in granite slabs, leads down through the trees to the road at Sous L'Eglise. At the point where the road crosses a stream at the bottom of the valley there is an *abreuvoir*, a drinking place for cattle and horses.

In the parish of St. Pierre-du-Bois an attractive walk connects the parish church with the cliffs of the south coast, a mile and a quarter away. Starting at Les Buttes, the medieval archery ground next to the church, it begins as a surfaced lane, then turns south and becomes a footpath, Le Chemin de L'Eglise, which cuts across the fields to the coast. As it approaches the cliffs it runs along the shoulder of a gorse-covered valley, while far below the sea opens out in front. The path ends at Le Prévôté, below a brooding concrete observation tower, built during the German occupation on the site of a Napoleonic watch house.

In Guernsey's largest parish, the Castel, the church is sited on the extreme boundary of the parish, while most of the green lanes radiate from King's Mills, a group of old farms in the centre of the parish. Folklore has it that the position of the church was selected by the fairies, who for some reason disapproved of the site originally chosen near King's Mills. Every morning the builders found that their tools and materials had been moved a mile up the hill. Eventually they gave in and built the church there.

An alternative explanation for the position of the Castel Church is that it took over a site of pre-Christian worship. In the nineteenth century a stone menhir in the form of a female figure was discovered beneath the floor of the church. She now stands outside the west door, where she has a splendid view over the northern half of the island.

King's Mills lies at the lower end of the Talbot Valley, which once contained a chain of water mills. The buildings are still there, although only one wheel is still turning. From the road the mill leat can be seen, following a contour on the opposite side of the valley.

One of the best lanes for walking begins at Le Moulin de Haut; there is a triangle of grass where the lane leaves the main road, After passing the mill it turns left and runs along the Fauxquets Valley, with a meadow on the left and a hanging wood of oak and ash on the right. Eventually it joins a metalled lane on the St. Saviour's-Castel border. If you go on a Sunday afternoon you will meet a few walkers, and you may even find yourself in the midst of a motor-cycle scramble. At any other time of the week you probably won't meet a soul.

Our winter flock of Brent geese has probably been here a month or two now, although I have only just seen them for the first time this season in the sea near St. Sampson's harbour.

The Brent is the smallest and darkest of geese, with a black head and neck, a grey-brown back and a white stern which flashes when the bird upends to reach something below the surface of the water. Adult birds also have a white flash each side of the neck. The geese are not much larger than mallard, and are often mistaken for ducks, but you do not need to be very close to see that the head is definitely that of a goose.

Brent geese breed in the Arctic tundra. There are two distinct races, distinguished by the colour of the belly. The pale-bellied race breeds in Canada and Greenland. Some cross the Atlantic to spend the winter in Ireland, and very occasionally one or two turn up here. All our regular visitors, however, belong to the dark-bellied race, which breeds in Siberia. In the autumn the birds migrate south-west to spend the winter on the shores of the North Sea, the Gulf of St. Malo and the Bay of Biscay.

Our regular flock arrives in September or October, and spends the winter pottering around on the shores of Guernsey and Herm. Their favourite food is eelgrass. This grass-like plant - the only flowering plant that lives in the sea in these latitudes - used to form extensive beds just below the low-water level of normal tides, and exposed at spring tides. There are still a few eelgrass beds around the islands, but the plant has declined everywhere in recent years, partly because of disease and partly from pollution. In East Anglia the geese have taken to invading farmland and grazing cereals and grass. This happens here to a lesser extent: in Herm I have seen them grazing in the field in front of Fisherman's Cottage. Mostly, however, they remain offshore. If there is no eelgrass they can feed on sea lettuce and other green seaweeds, or even small shellfish.

In 1981 all wildfowl received the protection of the law locally, and Brent geese have become more numerous since then. Opinions differ about the exact number. My guess is that about one hundred and fifty birds regularly spend the winter with us, with some of their friends and relations stopping to join them, on their way to some other destination. The largest flock is in Herm, where they graze the eelgrass beds around Vermerette and further north. At high tide they can usually be seen in one of the bays north of the harbour, off the common or in Belvoir Bay. In March 1994 I counted 95 of the little black geese, quietly honking to themselves on Bear's Beach.

On the Guernsey side of the Little Russell, geese can nearly always be found somewhere between Belle Grève Bay and Bordeaux, and groups of twenty or thirty can often be seen on the west coast at Grande Havre, Vazon or Rocquaine.

In April most of the geese return to their breeding grounds in Siberia, although some of the Herm birds are still around in May, or even June. They seem to enjoy the amenities of the island as much as we do, and are reluctant to leave. Some non-breeding birds may remain throughout the summer.

The robin is a much loved bird, especially in the winter, when its tameness and sweet song ensure it a place in our affection. One Christmas I undertook an ornithological survey of the cards on the mantelpiece. The robin was an easy winner, being present in well over half the cards. Snow buntings, geese and turkeys were definitely also-rans.

Not every generation has been so sentimental about robins. Dr. Thomas Muffet, whose daughter had the problem with the spider, adopted a more practical attitude. In his book *Health's Improvement*, published in 1595, he wrote: 'Robin red-breast is esteemed a light and good meal'.

At present the robin is one of the few small birds we regularly see in our garden, and certainly the tamest. Most of the garden birds are migratory to some extent and the individuals we see now are not the same as those that were here in the summer. The robin, on the other hand, is truly resident. There is some migration, for robins ringed in the Channel Islands have been recovered from both sides of the Channel, but most of our robins spend their lives in the island.

Although tame with man, robins are fiercely aggressive among themselves. In the autumn each individual establishes a territory, in which it will not tolerate the intrusion of another robin. The boundaries are established by a series of fights with the neighbours; the more aggressive the bird, the larger its territory will be. Having established its territory, it advertises the fact by singing from fixed points around the boundary. The song which is so sweet to our ears is a war-cry. There is also an urgent *tic-tic*. This is an alarm call, which in our garden is reserved for cats.

In the early spring the females leave their territories and pair with the males, each pair establishing a larger area which they jointly defend against all comers. Here the hen builds a cup-shaped nest of moss and hair in the ivy covering a tree or a wall, or in an old boot or tea-pot. The pair raise several broods until they moult in July, when they resume their solitary lives.

Being a mainly sedentary bird, races with slight regional differences have evolved in different parts of Europe. British robins have a slightly darker back, and the breast is a deeper red, than their continental relatives. But the main difference is one of behaviour. On the continent the robin is a bird of deep woodland, keeping well away from human habitation. British robins favour gardens and hedges, and are often extremely tame. Much of Guernsey's wildlife is continental rather than British, but judging by their behaviour, our robins are British.

There was a heavy crop of holly berries this year, and although half of them fell in the autumn gales, there should be plenty left for Christmas. The birds have not eaten them yet, being more interested in the berries of myrtle, hawthorn and pyracantha.

Long before Christmas was a festival, branches of holly were gathered and brought into the house at midwinter. Our ancestors thought it was miraculous that holly should be alive and green when all the other trees appeared to be dead, and gathered it as a symbol of life. Later, it fitted in well with Christian symbolism. The prickles recall the Crown of Thorns and the scarlet berries drops of blood. The white blossom stands for purity, and the bark, 'as bitter as any gall', represents Our Lord's Passion.

Today, when our gardens and hedges are full of evergreen plants collected from all over the world, it is easy to forget that before men began to introduce exotic plants, holly was the only broad-leaved evergreen tree in northern Europe. In the sub-tropical climate of the Tertiary era, Europe had a far richer flora than it does today. The plants were driven south by the arctic conditions of the Ice Age, but when milder conditions returned, only a small proportion of them found their way north again. Of the broad-leaved evergreens laurel, bay and rhododendrons still flourish around the Mediterranean, but only holly found its way back into northern Europe.

We know holly is a native tree in Guernsey, for its pollen has been found in the peat at Le Catioroc. Almost certainly it has been here continuously since before Guernsey became an island, and native holly trees are still quite common in woods and hedges. The nurseries have also imported numerous cultivated varieties, and most of the holly bushes in gardens are one or other of these.

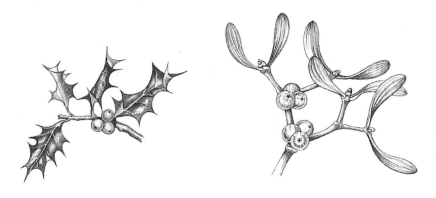

Left: holly; right: mistletoe

If holly was miraculous, mistletoe was even more so, for it remained green all through the winter, without having any contact with the ground. Mistletoe is unusual in being a partial parasite. It has green leaves and can manufacture its own food, but it has no roots, and attaches itself to the branch of a tree, from which it draws water and minerals.

It can grow on a variety of trees, but in Britain the green, rounded bushes are usually seen on old apple trees. Since old apple orchards are becoming a rarity, mistletoe as a wild plant is now an endangered species. In Guernsey it is extremely rare, growing only on a few old apple trees in gardens, where it was probably planted deliberately.

Mistletoe berries are eaten by birds, including the mistle thrush, although they must constitute a minute proportion of that bird's diet. The white substance surrounding the seeds is extremely sticky, and if the bird tries to wipe its beak against a branch, the seed may become wedged in a crack in the bark. Germination is slow, and it may be several years before a bush of mistletoe appears, often some distance from the point where the seed was lodged.

The connection between mistletoe and the Druids comes from Pliny the Elder, a Roman writer of the first century. He said that the Druids of ancient Gaul credited the plant with magical properties, especially when it was growing on their sacred tree, the oak. Since it hardly ever did grow on the oak, when found it was gathered with great ceremony. Pliny, who had a vivid imagination, described how it was cut by a priest in white robes, using a golden sickle. It then had power to cure barrenness in livestock, and presumably also in wives.

The connection with fertility has persisted to the present day, which is why we have a sprig of mistletoe in a strategic position during the festive season.

About the author

Nigel Jee came to Guernsey in 1952 to teach biology at Elizabeth College. Since 1955 he and his wife have lived at La Houguette, where the old farmhouse and large garden have demanded their constant attention.

Before long a house cow turned into a dairy herd, and eventually he gave up teaching to concentrate on the farm. Then he allowed himself to be talked into entering politics and for twelve years was a member of the States of Guernsey, becoming president of the committee concerned with agriculture, and then of the planning committee.

He has always taken a keen interest in the countryside, its wildlife and its conservation. He was a founder member of the National Trust of Guernsey, and later its Chairman. For many years he was botanical secretary of La Société Guernesiaise (the local 'learned society'). He has also served as its president, and as the editor of its *Transactions*. He is now an honorary member.

Since retiring from the States in 1991 his weekly 'Country Column' in the *Guernsey Evening Press* has chronicled the life of the countryside, as well as giving him the opportunity to ride his various hobby-horses.

His publications include *Guernsey's Natural History*, 1967; *Guernsey Cow*, 1977; *Landscape of the Channel Islands*, 1982; and (as co-author) *New Shell Guide: The Channel Islands*, 1987.